D0393024

INNER GUIDANCE
OUR DIVINE BIRTHRIGHT

INNER GUIDANCE
OUR DIVINE BIRTHRIGHT

Anne Archer Butcher

ECKANKAR
Minneapolis
www.Eckankar.org

Inner Guidance: Our Divine Birthright

Copyright © 2013 Anne Archer Butcher

All rights reserved. No part of this book may be reproduced, stored in a retrieval system, or transmitted in any form by any means, whether electronic, mechanical, photocopying, recording, or otherwise, without prior written permission of Eckankar.

The terms ECKANKAR, ECK, EK, MAHANTA, SOUL TRAVEL, and VAIRAGI, among others, are trademarks of ECKANKAR, PO Box 2000, Chanhassen, MN 55317-2000 USA.   120904

Printed in USA

Edited by Patrick Carroll, Joan Klemp, and Anthony Moore
Cover design by Doug Munson

Library of Congress Cataloging-in-Publication Data

Butcher, Anne Archer.
    Inner guidance : our divine birthright / Anne Archer Butcher.
        pages cm
    Includes bibliographical references.
    Summary: "Author Anne Archer Butcher's account of getting help in her daily life through divine guidance, dreams, miracles, and spiritual experiences in Eckankar with Sri Harold Klemp, the Mahanta, the Living ECK Master"--Provided by publisher.
    ISBN 978-1-57043-385-6 (pbk. : alk. paper) 1. Spiritual life--Eckankar (Organization) I. Title.
    BP605.E3B88 2013
    299'.93--dc23
                            2013001433

♾ This paper meets the requirements of ANSI/NISO Z39.48-1992 (Permanence of Paper).

Contents

Acknowledgments

This book is many years in the making. The fact that it is complete means that I owe sincere thanks to several important people.

First, a special thanks to Sri Harold Klemp and his wife, Joan, for their continued inspiration and for teaching me the true meaning of guidance.

To my husband, Alden Butcher, for his endless love and abiding encouragement—I thank you from the depths of my being. What a gift you are to me! Along with our daughter Sarah, whose love and presence in my life shows me a greater potential for blessings than I ever knew was possible.

And to Henry Koster, for your friendship, editorial support, and remarkable dedication to this project, always given with tireless service.

Introduction

*The purpose . . . is to try to give you an in-
kling of where to go and what to do to open your
heart so that you can have the guidance of the
Holy Spirit to help you in your daily life.*

—Harold Klemp
How to Survive Spiritually in Our Times[1]

---

*W*e all have inner guidance. It's the Divine speaking to us, to Soul, and it's always present in our lives, with us at all times.

Inner guidance is an exceptional spiritual tool. It opens the door of the heart to divine assistance, like having the wisest person in the world at our shoulder, helping with every decision.

Who wouldn't want that?

But for many, inner guidance is something rare and unexplored, available only to saints. That's why I wrote this book—to show how I learned about inner guidance through the fascinating teachings of Eckankar, Religion of the Light and Sound of God, and to offer you, the reader, ways to become more aware of this great spiritual gift.

The stories in this book are from my own personal exploration of inner guidance. I offer them in the hope they will show you the way to your own stories, your own realizations of this wealth of guidance and direction in your life. It's waiting for you to discover and cultivate for your own greatest good on every level—spiritual, mental, emotional, and physical.

I think of inner guidance as a GPS, a global positioning system that is all-wise and all-knowing, leading me not only to my highest purpose as Soul, but also to a destination far greater than what I imagine.

How do you begin using inner guidance?

The first step is to learn to listen, to tune in to the still small voice within. This was my biggest challenge.

Early on I wondered what would become of my life. I asked for inner help, and the teachings of Eckankar brought daily spiritual exercises. By practicing them I strengthened my inner connection with the Holy Spirit. I learned to receive and follow divine guidance in every aspect of my life—relationships, family, health, and career.

Now I can clearly see how inner guidance, the Voice of God, was directing the show. I have had more than one fulfilling career, I've travelled the world, and I have a wonderful personal life. I enjoy a deep love and remarkable marriage, a beautiful family, and a profound, personal relationship with God. It has not been an easy journey, but it has always been truly worth it.

I believe we can each follow our inner guidance from God wherever we are in life—no matter what spiritual path we are on. I was raised as a devout Christian, yet I was led through my own spiritual experiences to the path of Eckankar, into the deepest mysteries of life. What I learned through Eckankar about inner guidance, as well as universal laws and the secrets of the inner worlds of God, may be used by anyone regardless of background or beliefs. These heavenly gifts are available to us all. They are meant to uplift and transform our lives, completely and profoundly.

To truly understand the blessings of inner guidance, each of us must experience it for ourselves. By sharing these stories of inner guidance in my life—how I acquired it and where it has led me—I hope to inspire you to embark on your own personal exploration of our divine birthright.

We can all discover how to connect with divine wisdom. We can open our hearts to greater joy, love, peace, and success. And we can each fulfill our highest and greatest destiny in this life.

1

Learning to Listen to God:
How to Discover Inner Guidance

The Voice of God is speaking to us every day, in every way, in the smallest things in our everyday lives.

—Harold Klemp
How the Inner Master Works[2]

———————————

*T*he farmer down the road was the first person I approached with my question. During that summer, I often ate breakfast with him. "Do you know how to talk to God?"

Like all the others I would ask, he could only respond with gentle amusement, warm chuckles, and a little instruction on how to pray.

I assured him I knew how to say my prayers. This was something different—I wanted to really connect with God and to hear God too. Perhaps all my neighborhood friends that summer wanted the same thing I did, but no one could tell me how to hear the Voice of God and have a real conversation.

Deep down, we all know how to talk to God. It is simple, really. But receiving the gifts of inner guidance is not so much about talking as listening.

1

Listening was the lesson I needed to learn.

It was 1954, in rural South Carolina. I felt the desire for God stirring within me. What drove me to chat with my neighbors that summer was a distinct feeling that I had forgotten something important. It was like the fleeting memory of a dream that held a special key but, when I awoke, had escaped me completely.

Not knowing how to begin my quest for God, I turned to the people around me. I posed my childlike questions to my country neighbors, asking each of them, one after the other, if they knew how to talk to God. House to house I went, explaining how I felt—that I had forgotten something important.

My quest was simple: God knew what I had forgotten and would tell me, if I could just discover how to make this all-important connection. My neighbors were stumped and referred me back to my mother.

My mother helped. Mom told me that we all come into this world with the gift to hear the Voice of God, but the world keeps us so busy that we forget. She told me that at one time she felt that she had the ability to hear, but she had almost completely lost it. Mom reminded me that I must always remember to *listen.*

Certainly I did not know then what I've come to understand now. Prior to our birth in this world, we are guided by Divine Spirit to create a plan that will take us toward our greatest destiny. Surely God knew what I was here for and what my life was about—but I wanted to know too.

We each are Soul, and we are always connected to God—and yet we can become distracted from that intimate relationship by the routines of life. That was what Mom helped me understand. We must listen to hear the call and find our way. God is speaking to us all the time.

My farmer friend told me that if he had ever known how to talk to God, he had long forgotten. We built a friendship in our little talks that summer, and it filled my days with happiness. He made me feel safe asking questions and validated my quest. He told me that children probably stand a better chance than any of us to get in touch with God. Both of us seemed to want to keep that connection alive.

I wanted to fulfill my unique, individual potential and not forget who I was and what I came here to do.

In my early search for knowledge, truth, guidance, and direction, the farmer and my other friends continued to talk to me. They also wanted to hear the Voice of God.

My mother emphasized that in order to be able to talk with God, I would have to learn to listen better. She told me I would have to sit quietly and really pay attention.

Listening was not my strong point, especially as a child. But I began to work at it.

I began to hear the distant thunder as God's commands, the wind in the trees as God's whispers. I began to experience the breath of God moving the curtains in my bedroom. This was a first step, and years later when I began studying the teachings of Eckankar, I was happy to hear Sri Harold Klemp speak of God's voice being heard as sounds in nature—running water, thunder, the song of birds. The Sound of God comes through in all these ways; and as a child, just beginning this practice, I heard these sounds and assumed God wanted to talk to me just as much as I wanted to talk to God. So I listened.

Perhaps when we have a sincere, loving desire, we

can begin to connect more fully with the Divine. Gradually, I began to hear the Voice of God as insights that came from within, as well as in outer sounds. I began to receive small ideas and directions about my life.

Because I was listening, I could hear God's Voice speaking to me more and more clearly about both the important things and the smallest details of life.

Sometimes this communication came as an inner voice; sometimes I heard messages in the words of others or in the world around me. If things were not going well, I might hear words of encouragement. "Just wait," the voice would say inwardly, and I would know that help was on the way. Within minutes, the phone might ring, and there would be my dear, upbeat Aunt Joyce, offering a chance to go out on an adventure for the day.

My trust in this inner voice grew. It gave me an exhilarating sense of the interconnection of all life. *What could happen next?* I wondered.

*A*s we learn things, we make mistakes. We venture into areas that bring us intense lessons. It happened for me.

Trying to *make* things happen became my interest—not to simply listen for the guidance, but to direct it myself, to command it. This may be a stage we all go through. It gives us a heady sense of power, but it takes away love, and eventually it may stop the inner guidance.

Rather than remain in a happy frame of mind, expecting good things to happen and doing what I could to facilitate that, I tried to turn it into a magician's game. Fortunately, the guidance I received instructed me about this as well.

One day, I heard a stern warning: "This is *not* a game."

At a young age, I was learning that we receive those things with which we align ourselves. When we align ourselves with our highest spiritual good, we come into harmony with it and allow that which already exists to manifest in our world.

We do not try to connect with inner guidance so we can manipulate life or others. We defeat our higher purpose if we try to use this gift in that way. I am grateful to have learned this lesson early.

By expecting the best and surrendering this image of the best or highest good to God, we receive much more than we ever dreamed.

So as we express our desires, our greatest prayer might simply be, "Thy will be done." That is what we do if we want the greatest good for ourselves and others, and it is the way to avoid limiting ourselves and our potential. Always, our greatest good is God's will, even when it may not seem to be what we want.

Eventually, it became apparent that keeping my heart open is the way to hear God's loving voice.

Divine Spirit leads us perfectly, *if* we surrender to this amazing benevolent power. And this surrender is not like waving a white flag of defeat; it is saying, "I accept my highest good in this lifetime! I accept a greater outcome than any I might ever have envisioned on my own."

*A*s a barefoot girl playing on the red earth of South Carolina, living in the quiet farmlands of the South, my future may have seemed somewhat limited. But my inner guidance told me I would have a beautiful and fulfilling life.

God's voice reaches us uniquely, often through the people in our lives. My mother knew I needed to go to college, for example. "Life is not easy, and your education will help take you places," she insisted. So I kept that goal in mind as I grew up. My life was about to present more challenges, more refinement in learning to listen to God.

2

Leaving the Church of My Childhood:
Inner Guidance Brings a New Spiritual Direction

The search for God requires a deep yearning. Soul hears the Voice of God and wants to return to Its home in heaven. In the meantime, it's up to Soul, in one way or another, to find a path that gives the help It needs to take this step. When you graduate from one level of education in the spiritual works, God provides a step, then another and another.

No matter what path you are on or what faith you follow, be the best there is in it, be the cream of the crop.

—Harold Klemp
The Secret Teachings[3]

———————

*M*y family belonged to a Southern Baptist congregation. As a child, going to church was a highlight of my life. There, I could feel a sense of love and bathe in the feeling of being closer to God.

7

But by the time I was a teenager, those teachings no longer rang true for me, and I could feel the call to something else. It was a deep yearning I had to follow. I remained a single-minded seeker, always striving to find a closer personal connection with God.

When I was sixteen, I lived in Europe with my family. Because I could not speak the language well enough to clearly follow what was going on, I attended church services with a sense of openness to the spiritual feeling within each church I visited.

In some of the places of worship, I noticed a tangible sensation of love that seemed to emanate from the very walls of the buildings. Even before the services began, I could sense it. I was moved by this experience and sought it out in churches wherever I lived and traveled.

After high-school graduation, I returned to the United States to attend college. In the midwestern town where I went to school, I settled into a small congregation in a Methodist church. There were many things I enjoyed about this church. The people were friendly and loving, and the music was joyful and uplifting. I even became friends with the minister, whose words were positive and insightful.

Yet I continued to feel a divine discontent—a nagging feeling, a sense there was something more. I wanted to connect more strongly with my inner guidance. My desire to have a closer, more personal relationship with God was growing. Maybe it is a desire we all have as Soul, to connect more deeply with God and to understand the divine plan.

One Sunday morning, while sitting quietly in church, I began to receive an inner message. It was a booming inner proclamation—not a voice exactly, but rather the *sense* of a voice delivering a distinct message loudly and clearly.

This new inner message shot straight to my heart. It was a message of pure love, a characteristic of inner guidance that I have come to know and trust.

"There is something much greater than this, and you have earned the right to it. You must rise now and leave the church forever."

"Leave the church!" I whispered to myself incredulously. *I love church!* I began to panic.

I might not have liked what I was hearing inwardly, but I was certain of what was being said. This message meant that I was to end attending church as I knew it. With this realization, I inwardly challenged the voice, asking, "But what will I do if I leave the church?"

The answer came swiftly. "Go sit among the trees, contemplate God, and await further instructions."

I could hardly believe what was happening, but I found myself rising from my seat. As I looked around, everyone else in the church was standing too. Surely we did not *all* get this message! Ah, no, I realized—the service had ended.

Happy people streamed out of the church into the bright sunlight of this beautiful day. I trailed behind, savoring what seemed to be the closing moments in a long chapter of my life that had meant so much to me. Those life-changing words were ringing in my ears. I was being instructed to go and seek God and to "await further instructions."

An odd message indeed. Yet there were two things I could not deny.

One, I was experiencing a heightened state of awareness. Two, the promise of truth within this message was compelling and inspiring. If there was something greater, and I had earned the right to it, I wanted it! As a result, it was easy to accept what I'd heard. My inner guidance was carrying me above and beyond the clatter of any fear I might otherwise have harbored.

The minister was shaking hands with members of the congregation as they filed from the sanctuary. This Sunday I was the last person in line. The pastor smiled broadly and said that he wished to speak to me privately for a moment.

We stepped away from the others who were milling around at the church doors. He beamed at me and said, "Anne, I would like you to join me next Sunday, meeting people at the door after the service. You know that from time to time I invite someone to join me to have a word with our church members. I would be pleased if you would like to take part."

On any other Sunday, his invitation would have delighted me. Now it was too late.

"I just wish you had asked me before, because I would have loved to join you. But now I can't." Somehow I had to find the words to explain. "I am really honored," I continued. "But, as a matter of fact, I can't come back to church at all."

He was completely taken aback by my response.

"Are you moving away? Is that what you mean?" He looked disappointed.

I was reluctant to tell him what had just happened—embarrassed even. Yet a part of me actually wanted to share with him. I wondered if he might somehow be able to accept it, though I presumed he would argue heartily.

Gathering my courage, I began.

"I heard an inner voice at the end of the service. It told me that 'there is something much greater than this,' and the voice said that I had 'earned the right to it.' Then I heard that I must 'rise now and leave the church forever.' I was directed to 'go sit among the trees, contemplate God, and await further instructions.' I believe I should follow this guidance."

He would try to talk some sense into me, I was certain.

This kind, God-loving clergyman took my hand and moved us another step or two further away from any prying ears. "I don't pretend to understand what happened for you today, Anne. I, too, am sorry that I did not ask you to join me earlier. But in truth, I wish that I could join you."

His response took me by surprise! I opened my mouth to respond. He was quick to clarify.

"I don't really want to leave the church or this congregation; that's not it. I know that at this point in my life, I can't. It's just that I often wish I could find my own way—and I do believe there is something greater than this. You have a special path that is clearly waiting for you. That's quite a message you received. Impressive."

"I thought you would try to talk me out of it—out of leaving the church!" I exclaimed.

He smiled at me. "Some might say that is part of my job," he said, "but that's not what I feel in my heart. If you are being instructed by God, who am I to interfere? I would not want to, and I would not even try. I encourage you and wish you well."

My final blessing from this admirable man, it was delivered with a hug and a smile.

As I left his side, I realized what a great gift I was being given on this sunny Sunday morning. It was a portal to greater spiritual freedom. When I made the choice to follow the inner direction of Divine Spirit, this powerful inner guidance I had been given, even though it meant leaving behind the comfort of the previous ways and this beloved church, my friend wished me Godspeed and helped me on my way.

"*G*o sit among the trees, contemplate God, and await further instructions." In my ardor for God, I interpreted the inner guidance of that Sunday quite literally.

Every Sunday morning around ten o'clock, I would go out to the park near my home, taking a blanket to sit on and a little book that I kept as a journal. Inwardly, I asked for guidance and direction, and then I closed my eyes to ponder the Creator. Sometimes I would read passages from the Bible and contemplate their meaning. At other times, I would focus on a feeling of gratitude and allow it to take me to a new level of appreciation for life.

And yes, I received insights and awakenings. I would reflect on these and capture further realizations by writing in my journal. I began to connect with a deep sense of calm and happiness.

Perhaps this was the next step for me, learning to ask and then to listen. In the process, I began to learn to trust in God's divine plan and recognize the gifts in my life.

The awareness I now gained each Sunday was more personal and private than anything I had experienced before. It was like having a sacred appointment with God.

Later that year, when the snow began to fall, I would simply take a long walk in nature. Wearing my warm coat and boots, I strolled along the quiet paths and felt the love that flowed both to me and out from me. The park had become an outdoor cathedral where I could contemplate God and explore my inner guidance. Worship was now synonymous with breathing, walking, and being alive.

Many subtle changes were happening to me as I worshipped this way, month after month. The transformation in my consciousness delighted me, and the wonderful events that began to manifest in my outer life did as well. I knew the two were connected, and I felt that God was truly speaking to me, as I was learning to listen in a much deeper way.

I was discovering that indeed, listening is a powerful form of prayer. It might seem like an easy concept to learn and practice, yet it took time for me to really begin to grasp this lesson.

As I developed this rapport, making it my priority, significant inner and outer changes occurred. The combination of devotion and discipline that I was putting into these Sunday mornings was bringing me great joy. I was seeking and listening for the Voice of God in my life; and suddenly, everywhere I looked, I could see miracles quietly abounding.

*T*he synchronicity of life sometimes startled me; sometimes it made me laugh aloud. Now I could certainly see that life was interconnected, with all aspects working for the greatest good.

Sitting in the park one Sunday morning, I watched a family walk by. The young girl asked her father, "Why do birds fly?" He laughed. "Because they can. Wouldn't you want to fly if you knew you could?" I laughed too. Well, yes, perhaps that is *why* birds fly—because they can! I interpreted this little conversation, however, as

God speaking to me.

I later learned in Eckankar that this is called the Golden-tongued Wisdom. It is one of the more common ways God speaks to each of us. A key form of inner guidance, it can help us steer a better course for ourselves in both the big and seemingly insignificant moments of life.

Did this little family bring me a spiritual lesson that morning? A robin flew by, and I smiled. Why would we pursue spiritual truth in all things, in all ways, learning to listen and to follow our inner guidance? Because we can! Indeed, who would not want to learn to listen to God if they knew they could?

If we knew inner guidance and truth were all around, most of us would be grateful for the help. I was. To me, it was like the freedom of flying.

Those early days after I left the church of my childhood were all about learning this: how to open my spiritual ears, how to hear the Voice of God in whatever way It came. I was learning how much God loves me, how Divine Spirit was indeed working on my behalf to help me grow spiritually.

3

Portal to an Inner Library:
Inner Guidance
Reveals Mysterious Quotes

Whenever something out of the ordinary comes up—a deviation from the humdrum, routine activities that account for most of your life—it is bringing you a spiritual lesson. It is up to you to take the trouble to try to recognize what this lesson could be.

—Harold Klemp
The Eternal Dreamer[4]

We come alive when we are passionate about what we do. When I first began teaching high school, I fell head over heels in love with my career.

I enjoyed everything about it, from engaging the students in discussion to finding creative ways to capture and hold their attention. Teaching is by no means an easy task. I began my career when I was twenty-one, and most of my students were juniors and seniors in high school, just a few years younger than I was. But I loved it all. Because our ages weren't so far apart, I could easily relate to the students. I felt full of enthusiasm and energy and wanted to put new ideas into action.

My goal was to be the best teacher I could possibly be. However, since life does not come with an instruction manual, I found it challenging. I leaned heavily on my ability to listen for and receive inner guidance—what I'd been practicing since my early years in South Carolina. I decided to use the inner guidance that came through to enhance my teaching experience.

This decision required me to go well beyond fear into trust. In this stage of my apprenticeship with inner guidance, I gained an increasing awareness of the grand design of my life. And as I did, a great spiritual opportunity came my way.

It happened during my second year of teaching. I was employed by a small-town suburban high school in the Midwest, and life was very full. I was teaching during the day, working on my master's degree at night.

My classroom was large. Chalkboards covered three walls, and the fourth was all windows. Teaching American literature, I emphasized writers like Ralph Waldo Emerson and Henry David Thoreau.

To prepare myself for the challenges of each day, I offered a simple little prayer: "Dear God, please show me what to teach the students. Teach me truth so that I may better teach them." I then listened carefully to any inner guidance or subtle nudges I might feel as I went through my day.

We often talked about the beliefs of outstanding writers, and that led to periods of animated discussion and debate. I yearned to help these students find elements of philosophy that would assist them in their lives. I also recognized that what I taught them could shape their thinking for a lifetime. During each class, after we covered the primary material, I would write a quote from some noted philosopher on the board and invite discussion.

One day, the first of many unusual things occurred.

As I put my piece of chalk to the board, a mysterious feeling came over me. My hand moved across the chalkboard, writing a short line of text. I was writing something that I did not recognize. I could not recall ever having read these words before. What appeared on the chalkboard was this:

"My opinion is that in the world of knowledge the idea of good appears last of all, and is seen only with an effort; and, when seen, is also inferred to be the universal author of all things beautiful and right, parent of light and of the lord of light in this visible world."

What is this? I thought, staring at the white marks on black. *I did not intend to write these words! Whose words have I written?*

I backed away from the chalkboard, as much to distance myself from such an oddity as to study it better. These words had come to me through the inner guidance I had learned to trust so well. Was something wrong, or was something very right?

I felt uneasy, almost frightened. Yet, in the face of this uncertainty, I found a little comfort in the fact that the words somehow seemed familiar to me. Perhaps I *had* read it somewhere once and now, somehow, had spontaneously recalled it.

But who wrote it?

I placed quotation marks at the beginning and end of what I had written, but I cited no author as I normally would have.

Gathering my composure, I calmly announced to

the class that we would read this quote and then discuss it. Slowly I read the lines again. We were studying American literature, but this was not from any of the American literature I had studied.

Immediately, two students' hands shot up, and the questions began.

"Who wrote that?" demanded one student.

The other asked, "Are you going to give the author and the source?"

To cover my lack of information, I told my class that I would not reveal the author or the source at this time. We would simply discuss what was on the board.

Shortly, however, the bell rang, and the students left the class, smiling. They felt I was up to something. I reassured myself that I would do some research and find the source of the quote. The next group of students entered the room and took their seats as I hurriedly copied the quote from the board to my own journal.

Categorizing what had happened as an enigma, I simply put it out of my mind for the time being.

Listening is not always easy; there are many distractions in life. That's what I had learned even as a little girl. And sometimes it is difficult to fully understand what we do hear inwardly. This is a lesson we all have to learn through experience, yet it is unquestionably worth our effort.

The next class was advanced English. Soon, armed with a quote from Thoreau's *Walden*, I approached the board again. As in the previous class, I prepared to write an excerpt I knew well, this time about the pursuit of meaning in life. Yet, Thoreau's familiar words were not what came forth.

What I wrote was a new paragraph, similar in tone to the earlier quote. But it was a different passage

altogether, on a different subject. I did not even understand the meaning of what I wrote.

What on earth is going on here? I wondered. Now
I definitely felt concerned. But, trying to suppress my
rising anxiety, I thought, *How foolish! I can't be afraid
of chalk and a blackboard or of my own brain.*

As I put quotation marks around the text, I again
announced that, for the moment, I would not be revealing the author and the source of the writing; it was just
for discussion. Again, the exchange was enthusiastic
and stimulating. This group of bright students managed
to do almost all of the talking with very little direction
from me.

Uncharacteristically lost in my thoughts, I puzzled
over this mysterious incident that had now occurred
twice in my classroom. I looked at my hand that held
the chalk. Did it suddenly have a life of its own?

*W*as I being guided inwardly to an entirely new
understanding of spirituality? Hour after hour, new
quotes appeared on the chalkboard for each new class.
I decided to keep the writings on the board. By the end
of the day, I had used all the boards in the room to write
the quotes that had come to me. Now quiet and alone,
I stood dumbfounded in my empty classroom, surrounded
by the prolific handiwork of some unknown fount of
wisdom, and marveled at what had just happened.

Something very unusual was occurring. Was this
inner guidance? If so, it was beyond anything I had ever
imagined possible.

Compelling messages, some long and some very
short, were pouring into my classroom, each seemingly
customized for a specific group of students. As much as
I might have liked to believe I was the author, I knew

I was not. How was this happening?

It was a great mystery to me, and as I drove home from school, I hoped I would eventually discover the answer.

By the end of the first week, I had no answers, only many more questions. Other writings continued to flood into my classes. The students were becoming very inquisitive. I knew I had to tell them something soon; however, I was uncomfortable exposing this mystery before I had more personal understanding.

Armed with a journal of all the quotes, I went on a search for the mysterious author or authors. I pored through books in the library. I was confident the texts must be there somewhere. I could at least guess at sources and pore through books. Then, perhaps, I would be able to solve the greater unknown—how and why I was able to receive this material and share it with my students.

It was a frustrating search. Realizing I needed help, I decided to contact a university librarian one afternoon. I presented her with my list of "quotes," with little explanation.

She took up the challenge at once. This was before personal computers and the Internet, but she had access to a university computer. She could input key phrases and search for a possible author and source.

Many days passed before I heard back from the busy woman. In the meantime, this new form of inner guidance seemed to be in high gear. Hour after hour, additional material presented itself to me, and I offered it to my students. They were enjoying the mystery and novelty of the quotes and the heightened energy in the classroom. The entire group would become hushed as

I wrote on the board while they copied every word into their journals.

When I finally received a call from the librarian, I was not prepared for what she told me.

"I found your quotes," she announced. "It took a while, but I found that they come from Plato—from the *Republic*, his *Apology*, and his *Letters*."

Plato? I was familiar with his works only in a most general way. Flabbergasted and at a total loss for words, I simply repeated what she had told me: "Plato?"

"Yes," she said. "And, if I may ask, I'm just wondering how you came upon all this, without knowing the source."

"The quotes were given to me with no references," I offered as an explanation. A weak sort of truth, but better than no explanation at all—especially since I wanted to continue to receive her help. "As a matter of fact, I have more," I said. "I was wondering how much trouble it is to do this research. I would be happy to pay you if there is a charge for it."

"No charge," she assured me, "and I am very happy to help."

Concern had turned to intrigue. The quest grew more baffling daily. The answers I now had in my possession plagued me with even more haunting questions. Had others before me experienced this phenomenon? Who could explain how passages from the works of Plato could be mysteriously funneled through an unwitting schoolteacher to a high-school classroom in Indiana?

And *why*?

At night, I asked God these questions. My dreams were rich sources of insight for me in those days, but no answers came. Only more quotes.

There were other disturbing issues as well. The students were definitely talking about what was happening in my classroom. Word was spreading like wild-fire around the school. Could these experiences endanger my teaching career in any way? I longed to share this remarkable occurrence, yet I was hesitant to reveal to *anyone* the bizarre reality of what was happening, lest I be judged inappropriately.

This school was in the midwestern United States, in an area of very traditional religious teaching. Most of my family were conservative Christians, and I had been raised in a conservative church. I had never explored the greater mysteries of the universe—not even during my university studies.

Neither my students nor I knew what was happening here, and I was too concerned to really talk about it at all. Despite a few powerful spiritual experiences and a growing awareness of my inner guidance, I remained a novice concerning mystical things, a new-comer to this arena.

A nudge was coming through, though: It was time to change all that, to make sure I grew better informed immediately about all things spiritual.

To accelerate my schooling in these unknown realms, I added a Comparative World Religions class to my master's-degree program to see what I might learn about the secrets of the universe. I took classes in the evenings and voraciously read everything I could find in the area of spirituality and spiritual experiences. I researched other religions, reading about many different beliefs. I read about the extraordinary experiences of famous Christians and little-known saints. I read about the paranormal and phenomenal. Yet my own mystery remained unsolved and unexplained.

I had not yet found the teachings of Eckankar, and nothing quite suited or sounded right; so my search continued.

As the librarian provided information, I presented the names of the authors and sources of the quotes to my students. Before long, we were studying writings of Plato, Socrates, Aristotle, and several lesser-known philosophers as well. The students did not mind the addition of this enriching material to their studies; in fact, they had become quite enthusiastic about it.

One afternoon, a student named Greg asked to meet with me to discuss the quotes. He joined me in my classroom after school. Instead of discussing the philosophy or the authors, however, he wanted to talk about where I was getting the material. I was as evasive as possible.

He stood there, shaking his head, as I tried to dodge a direct answer. Finally, he laughed gently to himself.

"What is it?" I asked. "Why are you shaking your head like that?"

"We know what is going on," he answered with a grin on his face.

My eyebrows shot up in surprise. "What do you mean?" I was anxious about his challenging approach. I asked as calmly as I could, "Who are 'we'? And what do you *believe* is going on?"

Greg's answer stunned me. "You're getting that information inwardly, directly in response to the questions that we bring into the classroom."

"Why did you say 'we' a moment ago?"

He remained perfectly calm as he gently confronted me. "There's a group of us. We've been discussing it for a while. We've noticed what's happening. We don't know *how* you are doing it, but we know *what* you are doing."

I began to feel a little caged in. I felt drawn to share more with him, yet simultaneously ill at ease. "And what is it that you *think* is going on?" I asked.

He replied in a relaxed and self-assured manner, telling me what my brightest students seemed to believe was happening. "You're pulling this information out of the ethers somehow. We don't know how, but it has something to do with us—with each entire class maybe. A group of us has realized that if we come to class with a deep question or problem—something that's intriguing us—your quote will answer it.

"If we collectively decide on a question," he continued, "your quote answers it even more specifically—not directly, but in a larger way. I just thought you would want to know what we've figured out."

Now I was more baffled than ever. To make my frustration even worse, I was speaking to a student who seemed to know more than I did. I was outmaneuvered by his straightforward manner and cornered into making a full confession. I wanted to know whatever he knew so I could add it to the little I knew and possibly be able to find some real answers.

Greg was a bit of a paradox himself—a popular athlete, he was also very bright and loved philosophy, poetry, and art. I liked him. He was perceptive in class discussions and original in his thinking.

We sat facing each other at my desk. Leaning forward, I sighed and spoke in a low voice.

"I don't exactly know what's going on," I admitted. "I don't understand it. I do not know where the quotes are coming from, and even though I now know who wrote some of them and what the sources are, I don't know how or why I am getting them.

"It's just happening," I said, "and I don't understand it at all. I put my chalk on the board, and they just seem to flow out!"

Greg laughed lightly at my plaintive confession and

the image of a hand and chalk with a life of its own. "That's what we thought," he said, looking at me sweetly. "You're not worried about it, are you?"

I admitted that I was perplexed—a little concerned by it all—and asked him about the group that had been discussing the events in my classroom.

"Do any of you have any clues as to *how* this is happening?" I inquired.

"No, but we think that we should start extracurricular research groups," Greg suggested. "For those of us who already kind of know what is going on, you could give us extra credit for going to lectures and classes where they talk about mystical, spiritual, or philosophical things, and we'll make reports. We ought to be able to figure it out pretty soon."

What a brilliant idea! My students were already earning extra credit outside of class for in-depth reports on literature and philosophy that they researched on their own. Since some of them apparently could see for themselves what was happening in the classroom, they could begin to look for answers. We had no idea what we might be getting involved in, but Greg spoke quietly to those who might be able to help, and our research began in earnest.

The reports were inspiring but not really fruitful. We learned about all manner of things, including many different teachings, beliefs, phenomena, and spiritual paths.

We discovered automatic writing, in which a person channels another being or spirit. I certainly was not "channeling" Greek philosophers. What we were experiencing in my classroom differed in significant ways from all the information we were gathering in our research.

My students seemed to believe there was an inner-world library which we were somehow accessing. We were being guided to information that was important to us all, based on what we were studying and what the students were asking. But what kind of a library was this, where you can gain access inwardly and find answers as if by magic?

And why me? And why this group of students? And what was *actually* happening here? And how? We did not know. Each answer only opened the door to more questions.

Though I had no awareness of it at the time, I was on an accelerated spiritual study course, leading me directly to the teachings of Eckankar. Soon, I would learn of these ancient teachings and find the answers to my deepest questions.

The spiritual seeker travels his or her own path to God, guided by the Inner Master, the Mahanta. However long it takes, however many roads are traveled, Soul always finds Its way home to God.

But I didn't know that then. I was only watching this very strange phenomenon take place.

In the classroom, it was as if things were heating up. The energy was astonishing and electrifying, and when the students entered the room, many of them could feel it. Word began to spread, and soon there were many students vying to get into my classes. The room became packed to overflowing, but no one seemed to mind.

The inner circle of students, those who were still doing the extracurricular spiritual research, began to notice something else. Their work was improving—in *all* of their classes. They all felt smarter, sharper, more inspired; and these students were earning better grades even in their most difficult classes. One of the students called it by a curious name. He said that the students in the class were all being "quickened," and that term seemed to describe the effect perfectly.

My professional career was just beginning, and my spiritual horizons were opening up rapidly. I could not imagine life to be any more exciting than when I was in the classroom.

I was being opened to a truth greater than I'd ever encountered. As Harold Klemp, the spiritual leader of Eckankar, writes, "If you're sincere, God's Voice, the Holy Spirit, will begin opening you to truth."[5]

$\mathcal{T}$he entire process continued to perpetuate the quickening within many of the students and me, augmenting our comprehension and abilities in ways almost beyond belief.

It seemed we could learn more quickly and easily and had a broader awareness of things around us. Some found that, when it came to taking tests, they somehow knew even more than they had grasped during study and preparation. As they took their steps toward preparation for adult life, they were being inwardly guided to answers and awareness beyond their intellectual knowledge.

Were they being guided by God? Indeed, it seemed we were all being guided by a benevolent spiritual force that brought only good.

"I'm acing math now," one young girl announced at my desk. "I have never been good at math in my life—ever! I am not studying more or being tutored, yet suddenly I really know what the teacher is talking about, and I am making good grades!" I was pleased at her success and the new accomplishments of many of the other students, but the big mystery was still not solved.

4

A Dramatic Welcome to a Life-Changing Teaching:

Inner Guidance Answers the Call of Soul

If you are in agreement with the Holy Spirit, which is the ECK, you will be guided in the direction that will take you to the next step.

Whatever you are going through today is training for tomorrow. You need today to reach tomorrow.

—Harold Klemp
Cloak of Consciousness[6]

At the beginning of the new school year, the phenomenon intensified. A student named Steve came to my desk one day with a sheet of paper. He placed it facedown, saying that I should not look at it until class was over. During class, I wrote a quote on the board about how important it is to be free and strong and to think for ourselves. It just flowed onto the board, beautifully written—a full concept. A lively and deep discussion ensued.

After class, Steve showed me the paper. He had

written a statement about how much pressure there is to go along with the group, to do the popular thing. He wondered if the whole reason we are here in this life is to learn to be individuals and gain a sense of personal freedom.

It was fascinating how closely the quote on the board that day seemed to address Steve's issue and answer the question that he had posed. The year before, Greg had already alluded to this process, and apparently the new students coming in were experiencing it too. Steve told me that this was occurring all the time, both for him and other students.

He came back to class after school to talk to me. He shared that besides seeing that the writings on my board seemed to answer questions held by the students, he had also noticed another benefit of the quickening—one that others had experienced too: Steve said he was getting along better with other people, including his family.

Yet, Steve shared a new insight. He thought there was some sort of spiritual portal in this classroom.

Like a land with a spiritually heightened vibration, he felt maybe our classroom was ideally situated to serve as a gateway into some mysterious inner worlds. I was not so sure about all that, but it encouraged me to have our special interest groups continue investigating spiritual matters outside of class.

I trusted that soon the missing pieces to our esoteric puzzle would be found and all would be made clear. My commission in the meantime was to stay open, trust God, and let the process of inner guidance continue to show the way.

The students' interest in our remarkable classroom experiences was further fueled by the fact that we loved the mystery of it all. The classes were full, and there was a long waiting list of those who still wished to participate.

Then, one day, the librarian called me about her research. Searching for the quotes to find the authors and sources had become a sort of game. I couldn't wait to hear what she'd share next.

"I'm sorry to bother you, but for a while now we have been searching for your last few quotes. So far, no one has been able to find a source for this recent material," she explained. "Did you give us everything you have?" she asked. "Could you have any more clues you may have forgotten—or that you are willing to share?"

Now I was even more bewildered. How could the source of this material suddenly *not* be found?

Considering the massive resources they had available, this did not make sense. And we had been doing so well! My librarian friend promised to continue her search, yet her efforts remained fruitless. Week after week, I sent more quotes but received no positive replies.

I began to wonder once again if I could be writing the material myself.

Even the students questioned me. One astute young girl thought she had it figured out. "Are you sure you're not writing this? Couldn't you actually be the author, even though your conscious mind does not know?"

But as the information continued to stream into the classroom, I was more certain than ever that this was not true. I was not the author of this material any more than I had been the author of the quotes from the ancients.

Several students and I now gathered informally before or after school and discussed it. The students had latched onto Steve's theory—that indeed a portal had opened into this classroom from some secret, inner library. It sounded like science fiction, but we had no other explanation, and they favored this one.

Was this how other authors received their material? Was it why people say there is nothing new under the sun? Who knew?

Perhaps all the knowledge of the universe was hidden away, only to be exposed by writers who found the secret to mining it. Was I mining this material in some way? Did that actually make me the author, or at least *an* author, as some students believed?

No, I was not getting ideas or philosophy like other authors. I was receiving exact quotes that often I could not even understand.

One thing was very clear: we still had more questions than answers.

For weeks, a tooth had been bothering me, and I needed to visit the dentist. Unfortunately, the doctor had no appointments available in the evening, so I was forced to take time away from school. Reluctantly, I scheduled a time to see him during the day and asked the school to bring in a substitute teacher only for the afternoon. I prepared worksheets for the students— material that we would discuss the following day. This way, the substitute would only have to hand out the papers and let the students work on them.

The substitute, Mr. Adams, a young man I had never met before, arrived over an hour early. I tried to direct him to the teacher's lounge to wait until I left, but he did not want to go. He explained he came early to observe my class so he would be better prepared.

"How conscientious," I agreed.

However, the group he would teach was one of my most advanced classes, where the so-called quickening was most evident. I regularly received lengthy quotes for the board during this class. Because of the writing that I would not be able to explain, I tried to discourage him from coming to observe. I told him the classes he would supervise would be quite different from the one that was about to begin. I asked him again to go to the lounge and wait.

"Please?" was all he said. I was not happy about it, but he was so polite and insistent, what could I say? I asked him to sit *quietly* in the back of the classroom.

But at the first opportunity, Mr. Adams raised his hand to ask a question. Impatiently, I asked what he needed. Bright-eyed and full of interest, he questioned me: "Just curious! Who is the author of these quotes, and where did you find the information?"

Trying to avoid answering his question, I was somewhat curt. I gently reminded him that he had agreed to sit in the class and simply observe. But he would not be dissuaded and continued to press me for an answer. The students appeared very tolerant of his presence. Our Mr. Adams was like an innocent child in a room full of adults who all knew so much more than he.

An answer of some sort was necessary. "I read it somewhere and can't remember the authors." I knew this was certainly an understatement, at best, but it was the only answer I was comfortable providing. "We're just studying the content—the philosophy."

To my frustration, Mr. Adams wasn't satisfied and persisted. "But do you remember the book at all," he asked, "or where you read this material?"

Since many in this class knew enough of what was going on to recognize my bold deception, this teacher's persistence caused a little snicker from the students. By now, Mr. Adams could see that he was the only one who did not understand. Clearly, we were withholding something.

This was the worst possible scenario. Ours was a

very conservative community, and somehow we managed to carefully safeguard the spiritual aspects of what was happening in our little world. I now had to leave my afternoon classes to a man who was extremely inquisitive and who undoubtedly knew I was trying to conceal something from him. I lost my patience and simply put an end to his questions by telling him again that he was welcome to go to the lounge.

"I'll stay," he quietly replied.

Walking to the board to write a simple assignment for my class, suddenly I was inspired. Contrary to my intention, I quickly found myself writing a new quote on the board, almost before I knew it. I didn't want Mr. Adams to experience this, and was struggling inwardly, but it was going to happen anyway. Then I lost any desire to stop myself. For some reason, I felt clearly guided and safe.

The energy was intense in the classroom. The students were absolutely silent. All you could hear was the scratch-scratch sound of writing throughout the entire room. I glanced at Mr. Adams. His eyes were open wide, but he said nothing. I wrote and then stood back to admire this mysterious handiwork:

"We are all one Spirit; we should regard ourselves as a living part of the infinite life, and we must express divinity in each moment of our lives. Therefore, we are each a spark radiating from the great being called God."

It sounded kind of like Emerson, so I spoke about it from the perspective of transcendentalism. My students hurried to finish copying it in their journals. Ever mindful of the presence of the visitor in our midst, we managed to have an excellent discussion of this quote. My face burned with the energy in the room. One of the students offered to open a window. The room seemed blazingly hot!

After giving the students an assignment to work on, I dismissed the class at the end of the hour. Filing out, many of them gave me little furtive smiles, but the group was uncharacteristically quiet. I nodded in acknowledgement of what none of us would say.

Something strange had happened here. The energy in the room had been *far* more intense than ever before. One of the most profound of all the experiences had just taken place; it was as if a great reservoir had just opened energetically. And we had a substitute teacher sitting there, watching the entire event.

Or, by some means, was he actually a secret participant who somehow had served to *heighten* the energy?

At the end of class, I handed Mr. Adams the sheets that he was to give to the last two classes. I told him the yearbook group would be coming to use the room at the end of the school day, but that another teacher would be monitoring them. I avoided looking him in the eye and kept our conversation to a minimum.

He asked no more questions, and I left.

$\mathcal{W}$hen I arrived at school the next day, I was anxious, concerned about Mr. Adams. Some of my students greeted me just inside the doors of the school, so I asked about the substitute and what had happened in my classes after I left.

"Did he follow the lesson plans I gave him and provide everyone with the handouts?" I asked as casually as possible.

"No, he didn't do *any* of that," one student answered.

"Then what did he do?"

With a big smile, this student tried to explain what had happened. "He asked us all about you and the quotes on the board and wanted to read our journals."

"What!" The students were generally very private with their journals. I could hardly believe they would offer them up to this complete stranger. "Did you actually let him read your journals?"

"Yes, and he loved it."

I moaned. "What makes you think that?" I asked with a heavy heart, ever mindful of the conservative community in which we lived.

"He said he had heard about things like this before, but he had never seen it himself. After school he left, but then he came back while the yearbook class was meeting and brought you a present."

"A present?" I asked suspiciously. "What kind of present?"

Another student volunteered. "We don't know what it is. He had wrapped it up, and he put a letter on top and sealed it."

By now we had arrived at my classroom, and there on my desk lay the gift from Mr. Adams. With the exuberant encouragement of the students, I opened the letter first.

In it, he explained that there are unseen spiritual masters who work with people inwardly for years before they ever reveal themselves outwardly. He said that he had read about this kind of thing but had never fully comprehended it until he visited my classroom. These masters guide, protect, and instruct us for our spiritual evolution. He said he was delighted to see the quotes around the room and told me that he thought I would be pleased with the underlined passages in the book he was giving me.

I ripped open the package next and turned the book faceup so I could read the title. It was *ECKANKAR—The Key to Secret Worlds*.

"Eckankar? I have never heard of this," I said quietly.

"I have never heard this word before at all. Does anyone know this word, *Eckankar?*"

Puzzled students shook their heads. No one had heard of this word. There was hushed anticipation all around as I opened the book to the pages that Mr. Adams had marked for me. I read the boldly underlined passages on certain pages. Then I looked around my room, on the walls and on the chalkboards. There they were, almost word for word—quote after quote. And yesterday I had duplicated one of these very same passages on the board, right in front of the substitute teacher.

An inner voice of reason came from one of the students. "Let's read it! Maybe the answers are in the book. Shall we read it?" she asked cheerfully.

We all agreed, and read it we did. I stopped writing on the board and started reading aloud from this book at the end of every class. We read after class and before class. We read the chapters over and over again.

In conducting our spiritual research, we had collected a large number of mystical and metaphysical books which now lined shelves in the classroom. Yet we all agreed that nothing even came close to this new book. Each riveting chapter brought wisdom, insights, and ideas that we had only begun to explore from the quotes around the room.

We read the intriguing paragraphs over and over again, and always they seemed new. The book seemed enchanted to us; it was like a fountain of wisdom.

Here we had a collection of all the truths in the universe in one small book. The author's writing had an otherworldly quality to it, an energy all its own. And the material answered so many of our questions. The presentation of the information was inspirational and poetic. The students and I all agreed on this. We loved it!

The book told very little about the author, a man

named Paul Twitchell, and provided no way for us to find out more about him or this teaching called Eckankar. I began to do some research with my librarian friend and finally discovered that Paul Twitchell had passed away in 1971—several years earlier. That was all I could find. I gave her the title of the book, and she was going to try to find a copy for herself.

At first, I was too absorbed in the book to think of it, but weeks later it finally dawned on me that I should contact the substitute teacher to at least thank him— and maybe find out what else he knew. Yet, he was nowhere to be found. Apparently, he had moved right after I met him.

All we had was the book—our one outer link to a greater understanding of the mysteries of life.

*M*any things happened in quick succession after I read the book by Paul Twitchell. My spiritual experiences began to mount as I pored through the book again and again. I applied myself to the spiritual exercises I read about and rejoiced in the results.

And things happened in my outer life as well. My spiritual gains were reflected throughout my professional and personal life. I won an educational grant in journalism, and I was paid to accompany my very excited high-school journalism staff to a summer program at a major university. We all received scholarships for further study. The students won all the top awards, and our school gained recognition. I made enough extra money to take a carefree vacation, and life was delightful.

While I was on vacation, I carefully reread *ECKANKAR—The Key to Secret Worlds*, looking for clarification of many of the mysteries I had been experiencing. From it, I gleaned an understanding of the timeless principles of Eckankar, an ancient spiritual path. I marveled at how much of life was illuminated with such simplicity. Mysterious and lofty though it might have seemed, it now made wonderful sense to me. Through my own experience, I had seen many of the principles found in this book illustrated in my life.

I now understood the quote-writing phenomenon in the classroom as a form of inner guidance. As I offered a simple prayer to be shown truth each day before entering the classroom, I was helping to open a door to great wisdom. Now I was beginning to see that there was inner guidance for my every move.

But I did not yet know that Eckankar, with all the wisdom and blessings it brought, was part of something even bigger—that it was an ancient path emerging as a modern spiritual teaching, and that it answered the call of Soul for greater truth.

God was leading me down this road to discovering more of who and what I am, as Soul. And my next step was to begin resolving karmic conditions—past memories and debts that held me back from fulfilling my spiritual mission.

5

You Will Have a Child Before You Are Thirty:
Inner Guidance and Prophecy

Once an individual makes a commitment to hold true to the teachings of ECK and follow the words of the Living ECK Master, it is a sure thing he will see his outer life run in new directions. The Law of Destiny, which has dictated the direction of his life to this point, is dismantled. The power is taken from that mechanism. A whole new chapter is begun when the Master turns the page in the Book of Life.

—Harold Klemp
The Spiritual Laws of Life[7]

---

*N*o one asks you to follow the path of Eckankar or make a commitment to these spiritual studies. You may hear about the ECK teachings from a friend or loved one, or you may read a book or attend a presentation for the public; yet following this path is always a choice you make for yourself with absolute spiritual freedom. It is a private and personal decision.

When we make that decision, in many respects that is when the fun begins. My life may have looked topsy-turvy to some people, but to me it was exciting, intriguing, and full of spiritual blessings.

Yet imagine my bewilderment when, sitting at a stoplight after school, an inner voice announced, "You will have a child before you are thirty, and it will change your life!"

A wave of sadness filled me. I could not have children. Three different gynecologists had already explained this to me. I had made peace with it. Anyway, I was still single.

I sat there at the traffic light and shook my head from side to side. Alone in my car, I replied out loud to the inner voice, "Sorry, no child. I *cannot* have children."

The voice came again—inner guidance, loud and clear. "You will have a child before you are thirty, and it will change your life." The message was plain and deliberate. I did not hear it like an outer voice, but there was no mistaking the inner message.

Having a child was a long-held inner desire I had never examined. It was a wish I had never even considered possible, a dream I had never allowed myself to believe was achievable. So I was reluctant to give the inner sensation any credence. My response to this profound inner message, even to myself, was self-protective and glib.

"I wonder what *that* is about?" I questioned aloud.

A child? This inner guidance was beyond my comprehension.

I began to mull it over. Could it mean something other than actually having a baby? Could it mean a student—a child who would somehow come into my life and become very important to me? I was in my late twenties, so time was running out to have a child before

I was thirty. I would have to meet someone, date, fall in love, marry, conceive a child, and deliver, all within the next few years! If I were going to have a baby of my own, despite the gynecological prognosis against me, I would have to get very busy right away.

I laughed dismissively as the light changed and I drove off.

 ⌒𝓑y now, I had a working knowledge regarding inner nudges, subtle inner whisperings, and prophetic dreams of life. All wonderful forms of inner guidance, I believed they were a blessing and an important aspect of one's relationship with God.

I was happy to accept with gratitude the guidance I readily received, but I did not always immediately understand the intent of the messages. I was appreciative of the help and direction, yet sometimes a little confused. And occasionally, I did not like what I heard. Yet I was sure these messages contained wisdom that I needed, and I had come to treasure their presence in my life.

Every day the Divine reaches out to us, if we have the eyes to see and the ears to hear. I knew that, and I cultivated an even closer relationship with God via the spiritual exercises I learned through the teachings of Eckankar. They gave me a deeper understanding of how God talks to us in myriad ways.

But a baby? On that day, I would not even consider it further. Such a notion was completely foreign!

Besides, I had my career to think of.

 "⌒𝓣he school board would like to talk with you," said the principal's assistant.

I was about to face an unexpected challenge. Yet on

this day, I was not concerned in the least. I knew how hard I was working in my teaching career and what great strides the students were making. The school board must have heard how many students were petitioning to be in my English classes. They wanted to congratulate me!

At the meeting, the board members were very friendly as they invited me to take a seat. One of the trustees complimented me on another successful year of teaching. He told me the head of the department reported that I was doing an excellent job. I thanked him and said how much I was truly enjoying my work.

Then, without warning, the mood shifted. The chairman of the board informed me that he had also heard there were many extracurricular activities occurring in my classes. I considered this a good thing and eagerly nodded in affirmation.

But my enthusiasm was quickly deflated. Although the board appreciated all the extra work I was doing, they would prefer that I stick to the recommended curriculum. There had been questions recently, both from parents and from other teachers. What was going on in my classrooms? I was not being asked to answer that; the board chairman simply continued.

"If you will just teach the traditional curriculum," he told me with a pleasant smile, "the board is prepared to offer you another contract for next year."

The implication was obvious and shocking. If I did *not* agree to what they were asking, they would not be rehiring me! My precious job was in jeopardy.

Why on earth had there been complaints? Perhaps there weren't complaints; perhaps there was just too much energy, enthusiasm, and buzz about my classes. But no one wanted to allow me to defend myself or explain. Something was wrong, and I felt deflated and disappointed.

I tried to quickly sort this out in my mind. How could I agree to teach a curriculum that would have less impact and benefit than what I now presented? I was confident that my students were receiving enormous advantages from my classes. Some of these teens had been transformed from poor students, totally lacking enthusiasm, to excellent, highly motivated scholars. I longed to find the perfect words so that I could express to this board the efficacy of my approach to teaching. Instead, there seemed to be a gulf between my conscious mind and the shock that my emotions were experiencing at that moment. I did not know what on earth to say or do!

The board patiently awaited my response. I knew this challenge was linked to the classroom presentations of the mystery quotes. In those few moments, questions raced through my mind. *Do I actually want to know and teach truth? How much do I really want it? And at what price? How great is my desire?*

Suddenly and almost imperceptibly, I felt an inner nudge. I decided to follow this guidance. Based on my response at this moment, the school district would either support me or simply let me go for the coming year. I would be fired! But, could I find a creative way to express what I felt and somehow help the situation move to a new level?

I surrendered to Divine Spirit as best I could, and my mouth unexpectedly seemed to take on a life of its own. It was the exact sensation that I had felt in my classroom when writing the quotes on the chalkboard.

Smiling nervously as I addressed the school board, I thanked them. "I appreciate the compliments you have given me for my teaching. I am working harder than I ever imagined possible, and yet I truly love it. I am certain that if you knew and understood how much I am giving to my students and to my career, you would never want me to do less. I couldn't possibly give less than my best, and I am sure you would not ask that of me. Besides, I do not have it in my nature to do that.

"I am confident that if you really understood what was happening in my classes, you wouldn't ask me to do *anything* differently. I am also sure that if you do not want me here, someone else *will* want and appreciate what I have to offer. At any rate, the choice is yours. I continue teaching as I have been trained—to be the best I can be—or I go elsewhere. Please let me know what you decide. I thank all of you for the opportunity to meet like this!"

After shaking hands with the chairman of the board, I turned and walked out of the meeting.

The ball was back in their court. I felt very pleased about the meeting, until I'd walked out the door. Then my rational mind kicked in, and the realization of what I'd just done hit me. Teaching jobs were scarce all over the country, and I had very possibly jeopardized my contract for next year. Maybe I had even resigned! I really wasn't sure.

*A*fter that, I didn't think anymore about the inner message about having a child. I just focused on the school year ending and on cleaning up my classroom. Good-byes were said for the summer. I went through the motions of the last few days in a zombielike state. No word had come from the school board.

With classes over, I could have enjoyed the luxury of being at home all day. Instead, I just sat on my bed and cried. It was a difficult time, a period of soul-searching.

I wondered aloud, "How can this possibly work out well? Do I have to find a new school? Dare I still trust this voice within me?" Two startling messages had come through lately: first, about the baby, and now this unconventional guidance on how to handle the school board.

With all my heart, I wanted to trust my inner guidance. It was growing inside me, blossoming with my spiritual studies, and I longed to believe that I could stay in the same school and have a new teaching contract.

But as the days passed and no call came in, I began to wonder what I would do next. My rational mind urged me to call the school and beg for my job. But my inner guidance said, "Just wait."

I lacked the motivation to go looking for a new job, so I decided that waiting was OK for now.

I surrendered the whole thing to God. I let go. "Thy will be done," I told the Divine, and this became my guiding principle as I ceased agonizing and moved into a peaceful state of detachment.

Someone *would* want me. I had a lot to offer as an educator. I would stay open and imagine my new position as if I already had it.

I kept adjusting my attitude, little by little, to become more and more positive and more relaxed.

*A*lmost a month after school ended, the principal called. He didn't say hello or identify himself, but I recognized his voice at once. He went straight to the point.

"OK, Anne, what do you want?" he asked bluntly. There was even a little laugh in his tone.

"What do you mean by that?" I asked. "What do I *want*?"

We both knew what I wanted; I wanted my teaching position back!

"The school board would like you to sign a contract as soon as possible. They have asked to know exactly what terms you want," he explained. His voice was friendly and slightly amused.

Shock and joy both filled me at once, but my inner guidance alerted me to proceed cautiously. I quelled my urge to simply accept the position.

So I asked, "What are my options?"

"You can have whatever you choose," he replied. "The best classes, first option on grant opportunities, a raise, a lighter schedule—you name it. What do you want?"

I could not believe my ears. I would never have thought to ask for *any* of these things and would have gladly settled for just getting my old job back! Wanting to understand why this change of heart, I asked, "What happened?"

"One of the senior school board members has a son who attributed all his newly developed academic success to being in your class," he explained. "They want to make sure they don't lose you."

We waited in silence for a moment or two, as I listened quietly to the inner guidance I was receiving. Shortly, an answer came, and I said, "I don't want all the top classes, just some of them. I would like a mixture of students. I want to experiment with the various levels to see how I can teach better at any level. Yes, I'd be interested in applying for major grants. Please let me see what the possibilities are so I can apply. That would be great. And I don't need a lighter schedule. I will take a full schedule—as many classes as I can get.

"And, please, I will need full cooperation. I would be grateful to just be able to teach, and I'd like to know that you personally support me. I don't care to be concerned with the loss of my job. I would appreciate receiving the cooperation I need to do my work. It may be innovative and original, but my approach will always be professional and educational."

The principal didn't hesitate. As soon as I finished my list, he said, "I can do that, and I can get you more money too." I could hear the smile still in his voice. He then asked me to come in to sign my new contract for next year and pick out my classes, as soon as possible. Could I come today?

I practically dropped to my knees with relief and gratitude. I had achieved my goal and a whole lot more by remaining open, listening to my inner guidance, and trusting it. I was learning to follow it with a new level of spiritual conviction.

In the beautiful summer months that followed, I didn't hear anything more from my inner guidance about the baby. I decided it was a message about my teaching career. Little did I know how wrong I was.

But I had some other lessons to learn about inner guidance before the Divine brought me that far more significant gift I longed for.

6

Resolving Karmic Connections from the Past:

Inner Guidance Opens an Ancient Door

Each person will, in his own time, find the path that is right for him. And it may be many, many paths before he comes to the teachings of ECK. This is as it should be, as it must be, because God has made a path for every state of consciousness.

—Harold Klemp
How to Survive Spiritually in Our Times[8]

My courtship with my husband-to-be, Jon, happened at the speed of light. When we met for the first time, I felt that I already knew him. Sometimes that happens when we have karmic connections with certain people and we are just picking up where we left off. That certainly seemed to be the case for me.

Jon was the older, traveled brother in a family I already knew. I taught his younger brother and sister

51

in high school. Jon was a brawny carpenter who wrote me poetry and discussed philosophy with me. We were very compatible, and life was unfolding for me in another new and exciting direction.

We decided to marry. We would move to Bloomington, Indiana, during the summer and have the wedding at our new home. With daisies in my hair, on a gorgeous day, I married Jon on our front porch, with several friends as witnesses.

Just like any other young, newly wedded woman, I wanted my life to be wonderful and perfect. But soon after the wedding, a strange, unexpected feeling began to wash through me. I became aware of heightened inner guidance, warning me of changes to come. It was a premonition I didn't want to embrace. Yet, I was sure everything was as it was supposed to be. I was meant to marry Jon, yes. But my inner guidance was telling me it would not be as easy as I had dreamed.

My discovery of the teachings of Eckankar was just beginning, and I had much to learn about myself as Soul. And my very trustworthy inner guidance was hinting at this uneasy truth: I was about to face some important challenges along the way.

Bloomington was a lively college town. I loved shopping, every now and then, in the quaint stores all around the campus area, and I quickly found my favorite ones. I was especially attracted to Lila's Imports, a small shop with wonderful clothes.

One day, at the height of a downpour, I suddenly felt an urgent desire to go to the import shop. I was not normally so inclined to shop; sudden urges of this sort just never happened. I decided to heed the inner guidance although I did not even have transportation that day. I was at home, Jon had the car, and it was too far to walk in the pouring rain.

Undaunted, I called a cab, and out I went, motivated by my compelling desire to go to this particular shop.

The taxi delivered me to town in the middle of the storm. Rainwater rushed down the street and flooded the gutters. With a big umbrella over my head, I dashed through the downpour, across the road, and along the crowded campus sidewalks into the little building that housed Lila's Imports.

What a crazy day to go shopping, I thought. *There must surely be something really special waiting for me!*

As I rushed through the door and shook my wet umbrella, I was shocked to find that Lila's Imports had been completely redecorated. The walls were now painted a light shade of blue, and all the clothes racks had been replaced with shelves. The shop was now completely filled with books.

Was this the same place I had visited only a few weeks ago? I wanted to go back out and look at the entrance. The location seemed right, but the store was totally transformed, and I wondered why I had been in such a hurry to get there.

Several people were quietly browsing around. A young man was sitting behind a desk. I approached him and laughingly asked, "What happened to the import shop? Did Lila's move? And what is this place now?"

He didn't know anything about Lila's Imports. Apparently, they had relocated. Then he added, nonchalantly, "This is an Eckankar center."

Practically jumping over his desk, I leaned in closely to eliminate any unnecessary distance between us. I asked cautiously and slowly, "Did you say *Eckankar?*"

"Yes." He explained that this was a center filled with books about Eckankar, books mostly written by its modern-day founder, Paul Twitchell.

Eckankar had transformed my classroom teaching and opened a whole world of inner discovery, but I didn't know it could go any further. What a discovery! There was actually a spiritual gold mine of information about Eckankar, the teaching that had been dancing around the periphery of my busy existence. I began asking the young man questions on top of questions.

"I'm a new ECKist," he said. "Just a college student. I don't know a lot."

"What is an *ECKist*?" I demanded.

As he spoke, I held my breath. A major reality shift was taking place, without a single sign of fanfare. The volunteer college student told me more than I expected.

"An ECKist is a student of the teachings of Eckankar," he said. "*ECK* means Divine Spirit. ECKists are considered members of Eckankar, and they can study monthly discourses in classes called Satsang. I highly recommend it," he added. "But if you really want to know more, there is an ECK regional seminar tomorrow at the Holiday Inn. They'll be able to answer all of your questions there."

Now I understood the urgency to come out in the pouring rain, to this very place. I was guided here—mysteriously led here at just the right time to learn about the next day's seminar. First I had stumbled into an entire room filled with books on Eckankar, and then I learned that Eckankar is an organized teaching, and now I was hearing about a regional event where many ECKists would convene!

"What wonderful good fortune," I told the helpful young man. "I will be at that seminar." My heart was pounding. I tried to sound calm as I asked him to confirm what he had just told me. "So this is a spiritual path that people can join?"

"Yes. You can find out more about that tomorrow at

the seminar. I have a brochure with details about the event," he announced, holding the colorful flyer out to me.

I was not much of a joiner when it came to organizations, but I was eager to learn more. I took the information, thanking the college student warmly for his assistance. I browsed through some of the books, feeling that a grand future was opening before me. Since I was already mentally reserving the funds necessary to attend the Eckankar seminar, I only had enough money to buy one book, *The Flute of God* by Paul Twitchell. I could hardly wait for the next day to come.

Through half the night I read fervently, eventually falling asleep with the light on. Jon was open and understanding when I said I wanted to change our plans for the weekend. We had intended to visit friends out of state, but after I told him about the seminar, we readily decided that Jon would make the trip and I would stay home and attend the Eckankar event.

The next morning, my husband dropped me off at the hotel and left town.

The seminar had already started. I was late! The big double doors of the meeting room were closed, and I stood there in the hallway, unsure what to do. I wanted to go in, but if I opened the large door wide enough to enter, it would create a disruption. I hesitated and listened intently at the door, straining to hear what was going on inside. I could hear a speaker.

"Open the door," my inner guidance whispered to me. Something was irresistibly pulling me into that room.

I still waited several uncomfortable moments. Then I again felt the nudge, more insistent now: "Open the door!"

Despite any awkward interruption I might cause, I finally pulled open the door, slowly and as quietly as possible. Stepping into the packed room, I tiptoed down the aisle, looking for a seat.

The speaker stopped talking for a second, reacting to my entrance. I was slightly embarrassed but was certainly willing to endure a little discomfort for the thrill of being in that room. When the speaker continued speaking, there was excitement in his voice.

He was looking right at me as he explained to the audience, "And the woman I was telling you about just stepped into the room!"

Upon hearing that, I stopped in my tracks. I took a closer look at the stage. To my astonishment, there was Mr. Adams, last year's substitute teacher, standing onstage, looking right at me, in a hotel in this southern Indiana town, far from where I first met him.

It was a bizarre moment. Time and space seemed to collapse completely. He just stood there and smiled.

He had been telling *my* story, relating events from my classroom. Apparently, he included both what he had heard and seen for himself and what he learned from the students when he met with them while I was at the dentist.

The room was full; there was nowhere to hide. I just stood there, feeling a combination of shock and joy. I had been wonderfully set up by Divine Spirit. It was astounding to consider the succession of events that had to have taken place in order for me to walk into this room at this exact moment.

Tears began to stream down my face as everyone in the room now turned to see me. I quickly sat down in the closest seat I could find.

Instinctively I knew I had come home; such was the contentment I was experiencing. Standing in a crowded meeting room in that Holiday Inn, I felt more at home than at any other time on this planet. I had followed my inner guidance to this important turning point in my life, and it was as sure and natural as the pull of a magnet. And somehow, amazingly, these were my people.

Mr. Adams continued to speak. "If a person opens his heart to their guidance, the ECK Masters will work with a seeker and train him until he is ready to take a step onto the path of Eckankar. For this high-school teacher, that training was happening in earnest in her classroom when I met her and her students."

ECK Masters? Were there really spiritual masters watching over our every move, guiding and directing us to our heart's desire—if only we ask for their assistance? I had read about them in the book that Mr. Adams had left in my classroom some time ago, and I longed to believe.

My ears filled with a sound like ocean waves breaking on the beach. I knew this was the Voice of God speaking to me. I could hardly hear anything else Mr. Adams said. But it didn't matter.

When the talk ended, Mr. Adams picked up a guitar and sang a song that he had written about how we are watched over, inwardly guided, protected, and eventually led home. It was inspired by his understanding of Eckankar and the events he'd witnessed in his brief sojourn in my classroom. The song filled me with an overwhelming flow of love and a profound sense of peace and happiness.

*M*any of my questions from the past several years were answered during the course of that day.

I recalled the prayer that, as a high-school teacher, I had whispered each day before I began classes. The wording always varied a little, but the message remained the same: "Dear God, please show me what to teach them. Teach me truth."

By observing this simple practice, I had opened my heart and asked for guidance. Had the ECK Masters truly answered? Being taught from *ECKANKAR—The Key to Secret Worlds* would certainly seem to imply that.

Mr. Adams had told the audience that Eckankar teaches there is a living Master who is willing to help guide us all; there is always a living Master—the Living ECK Master, a teacher of divine truth. There were many things I was still in the process of learning and confirming for myself, yet I definitely wanted a greater understanding of these teachings. Fortunately, Eckankar is also a path of personal experience. You are not asked to believe anything that you cannot prove for yourself. Having already had some amazing experiences, I was all ears!

One aspect of truth that my students and I had discovered through the classroom experiences is that each of us is Soul and we exist because God loves us. Soul is an eternal being that has *chosen* to incarnate here to fulfill Its greatest spiritual potential in this lifetime. At the seminar that day, I learned that this was an important part of the teachings of Eckankar.

And I heard more about Paul Twitchell, an ECK Master who researched, gathered, wrote, and compiled vast amounts of esoteric wisdom, doctrine, and detailed accounts of spiritual experiences. He launched the modern-day path of Eckankar.

I also learned that my students had actually been right about the inner library I had somehow tapped into as I wrote the quotes on the classroom chalkboard. Truth exists eternally and is stored for those who seek to discover it for themselves. The whole story of the past and the future is contained within an inner library system.

This is indeed what my students and I had begun to conclude. In these great libraries in the spiritual worlds, there are source manuscripts from which we can gather material or access truth. I had already had first-hand experience with this.

On that day at the Eckankar seminar, inner walls came down. My heart was opened.

It became apparent to me that no one owns the truth. Though I had long sought its author, the wisdom that poured into my classroom did not need attribution. It simply was truth, revealing itself to those who were seeking it.

I was so grateful for this man, Paul Twitchell, who had followed through on his life's mission to bring the teachings of Eckankar together in one place and make it so simple and accessible to all of us. He had gathered the wisdom of the universes of God into the most penetrating study I had ever seen, and my students and I were given rare access to that bounty.

*T*his was the day, too, that I heard more about the Mahanta, the *inner* spiritual guide, serving all Souls with unconditional love. The numerous speakers that day referred to the Mahanta as the Wayshower who gives inner guidance and direction while allowing everyone complete spiritual and personal freedom. Because the Mahanta is an inner spiritual guide, he can be with every Soul at the same time, and he works closely with those who seek guidance.

"How do I join?" I asked.

"You can read some books and join a discussion group," the pretty, redheaded lady told me.

"I have read some books, and I would like to join now, if I can," I insisted.

She gave me a welcoming smile as I wrote a small check as a donation and provided my address to receive the Eckankar discourses I would study in a Satsang class. Those monthly discourse lessons and the spiritual exercises they contained would help me connect with the inner wisdom of the Mahanta. That day I became a member of Eckankar and could formally study these ancient teachings. I was giddy with joy.

When the student is ready, God will open the windows of heaven, and the Master will teach us, whoever we may be and wherever we are. Maybe, too, it's the other way around. When the student is ready, he or she suddenly sees the windows that are *always* open, thanks to God's infinite love, wisdom, and grace.

How marvelous that the Mahanta would take such meticulous care of the spiritual evolution of one individual such as me!

A paradigm shift had occurred in my life. I saw that possibilities are open to us that can change everything for the better. My life was being transformed and uplifted, and I felt acutely aware of the presence and gifts of God—more than ever before.

7

The Ocean of Love:
Inner Guidance during an Out-of-Body Experience

Whenever Soul reaches the far orbits of the inner planes through Soul Travel, the human heart opens to God's all-consuming love.
It is our very purpose to discover that love.

—Harold Klemp
Past Lives, Dreams, and Soul Travel[9]

---

*T*he inner experience was very clear. I looked out from the waist-high shimmering waves in which I stood, and I spied the huge, brilliant source in full flood. It rose up as high as I could see and fell like a breathtaking waterfall all around.

It appeared to be the magnificent origin of the ocean in which I bathed during this Soul Travel experience.

Like liquid light, its waters flowed out in massive golden streams, sparkling and incredibly dazzling. A beautiful sound filled the air. Mists of golden droplets floated around me, and I breathed in all that I could of this stunning essence, feeling tremendously blessed to be alive.

I stood transfixed by the scene of the glorious waterfall. Ah, if the world could only know about this exquisite beauty, this absolute peace, this breathtaking world of divine Light and Sound. It felt like home, a place where we all belong.

This world was now the only reality I ever wanted to experience.

*N*ow that I was a student of Eckankar, I was learning so much. Pure love is the essence of life, I realized; it links us all together for the good of everyone. Each day, I was being reminded how inner guidance can work not only for oneself, but for the benefit of others, especially our loved ones. I was experiencing, as I did in this contemplation journey to the mysterious ocean, the divine inner connection that allows us to know things and sense things beyond the ken of our everyday awareness.

Letting go and trusting the power of love is the heart of the journey we're on. At the time, discovering this level of love was a startling new dimension of inner guidance.

*O*ne night, a headache came on suddenly. I was getting ready to leave for the master's-degree class that I attended three times a week, but my temples were pounding like a hammer, and with each throb came excruciating pain.

Jon sat down on the couch with me as I became more lightheaded and dizzy from the headache. He sat holding me, concerned, wondering aloud if I needed to skip my class.

Missing a three-hour class was greatly discouraged. If it happened twice, you were out. Besides, we were expecting a guest speaker that evening, an international expert in documented mystical and spiritual experiences. He was coming to share his stories and insights gleaned from encounters with outstanding shamans, mystics, and revered spiritual men and women of various paths and faiths. I certainly did not want to miss that.

But a strange and powerful feeling was enveloping me—an eerie, cold sensation. I sensed the now-familiar, unspoken, yet perfectly clear, communication. My inner guidance was warning me about something, and soon the words came through, loud and clear: "Someone close to you appears to be dying."

I couldn't believe it. First, I turned to Jon and asked him anxiously, "Do you feel well?"

He laughed at my question. He felt fine. "Why are you asking me if I feel well? You're the one with the headache."

And indeed, the headache and the message seemed to be linked somehow. But how? Maybe I was not listening intently enough to the message. I sat very still for a few minutes, listening more carefully and trying to ignore the pain. Was someone dying? If so, who? And was there something I needed to do about all of this?

As a few minutes ticked by, I gained the impression it was someone else who was dying, someone *emotionally* close to me. My mind raced to figure out who it might be. I thought of my mother, so I walked to the phone and called her in South Carolina. All was well, and she felt fine.

Next, I called my older sister in New York City. No answer, but this was not unusual for her. Debbe was a high-powered executive working for an international banking firm. Her life was busy, demanding, and full. I imagined her out for the evening in the city, laughing with friends and enjoying herself.

I couldn't think of anyone else I should call. Maybe I misunderstood the inner message. Maybe the problem was actually with me. Needing relief from the headache, I remembered to send out a silent plea for guidance and protection.

"Please help me!" I said.

*H*arold Klemp writes, "Dreams, visions, and other experiences mean nothing in themselves. But in the context of our spiritual life, they are signs of how much we are in accord with life. In fact, the whole point of life is to teach us how to come into agreement with the Voice of God, the Light and Sound. Many find the road to their inner worlds through the teachings of Eckankar."[10]

As I sent out the silent plea for help, my attention unexpectedly was drawn to a dark spot across the room. I leaned forward on the couch and tried to focus on it. I hadn't noticed it before. Maybe the headache was affecting my vision. Yet with my eyes wide open, I clearly saw a black spot hanging in the middle of the room, about six feet above the floor.

I peered at it. The disc became even more distinct and clear. It was a small, pitch-black, circular spot, suspended in midair in my living room!

I anxiously said to Jon, "There's something you've got to see. Look over there. Can you see it?"

Jon leaned forward and looked across the room. "I see the stereo," he said. "What do you see?"

"I see a small, black spot hanging in the middle of the room. It's not my eyes. If I look away I don't see it. It's right *there*," I said, pointing in front of the stereo cabinet.

Jon squinted and said, "I don't see a spot. Do you mean there's a spot *on* something?"

"No, Jon. It's a *thing*! It's a small black thing, shaped like a spot or a circle. Try to focus and just look. I'm sure you can see it." I urged him to try harder as I stared at it even more closely. There was no doubt that it was real. I then glanced at Jon, wondering how I might help him see this strange thing. He was not even looking at the spot. He was staring at me.

"What's the matter? Can you really not see that?" I asked insistently. "Just *look* at it. It's right there in front of you. Please just *try*." But Jon was looking at me intently, as if he didn't know who I was. "Look at this with me," I pleaded again.

To get a better look, I tried to stand up and cross the room to gaze at it more closely, to really examine it. But I couldn't. My body suddenly seemed heavy and unable to move. At the same time, I felt that I was being pulled in the direction of the black spot—pulled out of my own body, straight into it. Not wanting to let go, I held tightly onto Jon. But holding on with my physical body did not stop the pulling sensation.

Certainly, nothing like this had ever happened to me before! I rapidly entered into the blackness.

Dramatically and suddenly, I crossed a threshold into a dark tunnel of immense length—large at my end but receding to a small, distant pinpoint of light. Everything occurred at terrifying speed. I felt freezing cold and in great distress, and I struggled to tell Jon what I saw. "It's so cold and dark. I'm going through a tunnel. There's a small bright light at the end, and I'm going toward it. I'm going so fast!"

I was aware of my body, shivering with the cold, eyes wide open, still sitting there on the living-room couch. I could feel Jon holding my physical body. Simultaneously,

I was flying through the tunnel at great speed.

*S*uddenly, everything changed. I now saw a brilliant light and, rocketing toward it, I felt great warmth as I approached. The feeling grew so intense that I became extremely hot. The heat seemed to penetrate every cell of my body.

All was dazzling yellow and then white, brilliant to such an absolute extreme that I was sure I was being blinded. Then an emphatic inner command flashed into my awareness: "Close your *physical* eyes."

Obediently, I closed my eyes tightly, and they no longer burned. Instantly, in this world of light, I could see much more clearly. While my body remained sitting on my living-room couch, I was also somehow stepping consciously into a beautiful ocean. It was golden and white, a vast sea, gleaming with incredible bright light.

Giant, sparkling waves rose and fell around me in shimmering radiance. A sound of the sweetest music imaginable seemed to flow right out of the source of this great ocean, from the dazzling waterfall. Swells of this magnificent ocean of light flowed right through me, filling me with love, beauty, and joy.

I held out my hand to test the waters and made a startling discovery.

"They are not liquid!" I cried, as the gleaming golden and white light continued to flood through me. I experienced a sweetness that was far beyond anything I could remember.

Oh, if only I had known! I would have lived my life with so much more joy, so much more confidence. For in this ocean of resplendent glory and divine light, I felt perfect, whole, and wonderful. I was cared about deeply, loved, forgiven, caressed, and adored. Everything around me was glorious.

My only desire at that moment was to stand in this pure ocean of love for eternity, to fill my being with the splendor of this setting. I neither needed nor wanted anything else. Standing alone in this radiant universe, I had absolute peace and contentment. Here, I would remain forever.

*T*his reverie was interrupted abruptly. Another inner message came to me like a loud, deep voice, saying, "There are ten things you must remember."

At that moment, I started to ignore the inner guidance. I did not care about remembering any instructions. I did not even want to be told what they were. I was complete and entirely content and wanted nothing to interrupt this joy, this divine bliss.

Even though I knew that life is about so much more than our own self-awareness and gratification, I didn't want to be disturbed from my experience. I knew that life is about love, service, and caring, and that if we don't master those lessons, it is doubtful we can ever pass the true tests of life. Yet, in that moment, I didn't want to put my attention on anything else. I had no intention of leaving this place. I did not want to hear ten things. Surely I would not need them.

Even if I did hear them and was forced to leave this paradise, I felt certain that I would forget anything I had been told.

But just as suddenly, I realized that my every word, my every thought, my every feeling, was known here instantly.

"You *will* remember *everything*," I heard.

And then, slowly, one by one, I received the following list of ten instructions. Each number was called out clearly. The delivery was precise and intense. I both heard and *felt* the messages going through me:

1. *Although you have absolutely no intellectual knowledge of what is occurring, someone very close to you appears to be dying.*

2. *In truth, there is no death—only the illusion of death.*

3. *However, upon learning of this apparent death, you must go at once to this person.*

4. *In order to help this person, you will be instructed and must follow these instructions.*

5. *You must tell everyone concerned, "This is not death."*

6. *After this experience, this person will be better off than ever before.*

7. *However, it will not appear to be so.*

8. *You must leave here when you are told to do so, although you will not wish to, for . . .*

9. *You have much to do. You must listen carefully and do as you are instructed.*

10. *Remember, everything is always happening exactly as it should, whether it appears that way or not.*

These words were flowing through the center of my mind, though my awareness was elsewhere. The voice was neither male nor female, but more like a mighty wind sweeping the words right through my being.

My heart was filled with confidence and joy, and I was moved to tears. Yet, as selfish as it may have been,

I still found myself indifferent to the message I was receiving and the ten things I was supposed to remember. As profound as they were, none of it mattered to me.

I had decided to stay.

Despite any higher understanding of life's purpose and my potential responsibilities, I could not help myself. Regardless of the clear directive I had just received, "You must leave here when you are told to do so," I absolutely did not wish to leave. As to the idea that there was much to do, I just wanted someone else to do it! Compared to this sense of fulfillment and bliss, instructions meant nothing, no matter how clear, no matter how important.

Like a childish Soul with only self-satisfaction as a goal, I shamelessly sought to think only of the beauty and wonder around me and the ecstasy flowing within me.

$\mathscr{A}$s I continued to stand in this grand ocean, I again heard the message resonating clearly through my head: "You must leave now. There is *much* to be done."

"Please, please, let me stay," I pleaded brazenly. Desperately I promised, "I won't ask for a thing. I will just stand here forever. Someone else can do the ten things. I won't remember. Just let me stay."

Yet, no resistance was possible. I experienced an instantaneous and abrupt sensation of being pulled away from where I was standing. A deep, primordial longing filled me. With every fiber of my being, I resisted the force so that I might stay in this place, in this serenity, for even a moment more. Yet, any effort was futile.

The last thing I heard was message number nine. Benevolently, it resounded in my head and heart: "You have much to do. You must listen carefully and do as you are instructed."

I was being sent back into the physical world, and the pain of expulsion from this magnificent and wondrous paradise was unbearable. I struggled to look straight into the sky of hazy golden light, to gaze at the brilliant waterfall, to cling to the feeling of joy and stay just a little bit longer, to remember the ecstasy I was experiencing. But I was being sucked back through the tunnel, traveling suddenly at breakneck speed into its freezing, constricted, shadowy depths.

The tunnel was as terrible as the ocean was glorious. Even the split second that it may have taken for me to pass through this black and frigid abyss was dreadful. The bone-chilling cold hit me once again. It was sudden and shocking, and for a moment I felt I had lost consciousness.

The experience of returning through the tunnel was so intense that my physical body began to shake violently. I was still shivering from the cold of the tunnel when I realized I was again sitting on the couch with Jon, who was gasping in disbelief as he held me in his arms.

"What's happening, Anne?" he asked.

On the verge of tears, I could not speak. Teeth chattering uncontrollably, I shook my head from side to side to indicate that I couldn't talk and moved even closer into the warmth of his body. After a few moments, I looked up at Jon and managed a faint smile.

This experience had shown me my true identity as Soul—the true, highest self that we all are—and I would never forget it. As Soul, we are radiant spiritual beings of love. I was so grateful for what I had just experienced. I now knew firsthand that there were wonders within the universes of God that exceeded anything I might ever have imagined.

Trying to comfort me, Jon gently patted my shoulder. Then he looked at my face closely and frowned. "Anne, something's wrong. What's happened to your eyes?"

He led me to the bathroom mirror so that I could take a look for myself. I squinted as he turned on the light. My eyes were light sensitive. Then I focused, and what I saw staring back at me was quite a shock. There was no white to the whites of my eyes. Just bright red! My eyes appeared to be completely sunburned, like after a day on the beach with no sunglasses.

If I needed any evidence of my spiritual experience, it was right here before my blood-red eyes. I heard the echo of instruction from just minutes ago: "Close your physical eyes." Now I understood its importance. It was to protect my physical eyes from the intensity of the extraordinary light in that tumbling waterfall of pure love.

As I slowly found my bearings and reconnected with familiar surroundings, I explained to Jon that I had somehow moved into a world that was more real than this one; that it made this world seem like a hollow reflection of all that life could truly be. Yet, I had also experienced a physical change while in this place, and however it happened, it was real, and my eyes bore the unmistakable evidence.

Jon was quiet and thoughtful. Collecting myself as best I could, I told him I was given ten things to remember and that I could still recall them clearly. I went to my desk and jotted down the messages I was given—one through ten—and I showed Jon.

"This is incredible! But I wonder how this could even be happening, Anne. And who is dying? Do you think you can figure out who is dying?"

"Whoever it is, the person is *not* dying. It's only the

appearance of death," I faithfully reminded him, "only an illusion."

Jon slowly nodded his understanding. This incredible experience had actually been about death, dying, and the illusion of death. My thoughts turned to concern about the person whose life was in peril, but the thought was disconcerting.

Still struggling to focus, I said, "I don't know who this person is, but I'm confident I'll find out, and then I'll just do whatever I can." Jon reassured me that he would help me if he could.

We talked for a few more minutes, but I could tell Jon was restless and ready to go. I couldn't really blame him, and anyway it was time for me to leave for my evening class. I reasoned that this would help me shift my attention and feel more grounded. If I hurried, I could just make it to class on time.

As I drove past the airport, a large jet flew over my car. The airplane, having lifted its great bulk at takeoff, zoomed overhead and soared into the night sky. I felt a surge of energy go through me, and I began to cry gently.

I pulled off the highway, parked the car on the shoulder, and allowed my tears to flow for just a few minutes. The tears provided a release from the intensity of my out-of-body experience.

Then I remembered another one of the inner messages: "Upon learning of this apparent death, you must go at once to this person." The jet flying overhead triggered the memory of the instruction, and I saw inwardly that I would need to fly to help this person. As soon as I knew where to go, I would have to leave at once. I resisted the urge to speculate about the identity of the person needing my help or to turn around and go home. I wiped my eyes, pulled back into traffic, and drove to campus for my scheduled class.

I slipped quietly into a seat near the back of the room and took out my notebook. Today's experience had caused me to feel that my life was beyond my own comprehension. I was feeling intensely vulnerable.

The visiting professor spoke only a short time before faltering in his presentation. He stopped, looked directly at me in the back of the room, and abruptly told the class to take a ten-minute break. Then he left the podium and walked toward me.

"Strange as it might seem," he said, "you have a very bright light all around you! And your eyes . . . Has something special happened to you? Do you want to talk about it?"

This is what he did for a living—he recognized spiritual experiences when they happened and documented them. Of course he would want to hear all about what I was experiencing.

In spite of feeling vulnerable, I had been eager to meet him and had come here ready to ask him questions. But now a subtle inner alarm went off, and I felt compelled to keep silent about the experience. It was not time to share.

As much as I wanted to hear what the professor had to say, I knew that I could not speak about my experience to him. It was as if I would be breaking some unknown spiritual law, were I to do so. I apologized, telling him that I needed to go home.

Although it was early spring and the weather had been warm for days, I awoke the next morning to a light snow covering the ground. The sun was shining brightly on this white blanket, and the world seemed refreshingly clean and peaceful.

This beautiful scene only emphasized what I was sensing: I had been transformed by the experience of the night before. I had a new and different perspective; I felt greater love for everyone and everything. I had stood in a vast ocean of love, and I was changed forever. I had returned as I had to, and yet it seemed as if I had never left at all. Had I been able to carry with me some of the mystery, love, and blessings of the heavenly realms of God? Now my world seemed blessed and beautiful, and I no longer ached to remain aloof and distant from life; I was glad to be back.

I was busy instructing my second class that morning, when the principal came in. He gently asked me to follow him and added that I should bring my purse.

"Am I going somewhere?" I asked him softly. "And what about my class? I'm teaching."

I sensed something foreboding in his manner. He didn't want to speak about it in front of the students.

"I need you to come to the office. Don't worry about the class." He addressed the students and directed them very patiently and simply, "Please continue."

He stepped out of the room and walked just ahead of me. I understood. Last night's prediction had begun its course. Somewhere, someone I knew and loved was close to death. And yet, I now knew that there is no death. That message filled my head: "In truth, there is no death—only the illusion of death."

I was about to learn the next level of truth about inner guidance, in a very dramatic and unexpected way.

8

There Is No Death:
Inner Guidance
Assists with a Loved One

We look for the Light, and we listen for the Sound of ECK. With these as our inspiration and guide, our pillars of strength, we can take any hardship in life; we can accept this life as an opportunity for Soul to reach God Consciousness.

—Harold Klemp
The Golden Heart[11]

I recalled the previous night's inner message: "Someone very close to you appears to be dying." Hoping I was up to whatever lay before me, I somberly followed the principal into his office. I was startled to find Jon waiting there for me. He had his back to the door.

Jon abruptly turned and spoke very quickly and quietly, "Anne, it's your sister, Debbe. You have to go to New York right away. They think she has only hours to live. The doctors don't believe she'll make it through the day, so they've been trying to reach the closest relatives as quickly as possible. Your mother is already on her way there."

After I'd left for school in the morning, Jon had answered the phone when it rang. My mother was calling to try to reach me and clarify what was going on. She explained everything to Jon, and he then packed some clothes for me and reserved an airline ticket in my name.

Mother had said Debbe was in the hospital and on the verge of death. Instantly, Jon had decided to tell my mother about the spiritual events from the night before, including my out-of-body experience and the list of "ten things." He read them to her point by point. Rather than being shocked by the message, my mother responded well. Jon said she seemed reassured from what she heard and had latched onto the most important detail: Debbe was not dying.

Sometimes our inner spiritual guidance is clear and precise. If we listen and follow it, we can be led to miracles beyond what most people ever imagine. My guidance had been clear. I *must* go to this person at once and follow all instructions, and this person would not die. So Debbe would not die, and this was just the illusion of death, and I must go as quickly as possible to her and help in whatever way was necessary. This was the practical application of all that I had been told.

I hoped fervently that all this was true and that my sister would live. I trusted my inner guidance, but I knew there might be room for some misinterpretation on my part. Yet there was no time for doubt, worry, or dread. These are often our biggest handicaps when learning to trust.

Encouraging me all the way, Jon drove me to the airport, and within hours I was with my mother in New York City.

Mom met my plane, and we rushed to Debbe's bedside. Following the fifth instruction, "You must tell everyone concerned, 'This is not death,'" I faithfully assured Mom that my sister was not dying. Mom's demeanor lightened. Just speaking those words seemed to convey the conviction of life and brought renewed hope and encouragement.

We arrived at the hospital where my sister was under intensive care. We hastened to her bedside, although the staff objected. The head nurse explained that the doctors did not know what was wrong with her and they were keeping her isolated. Undaunted, we persisted until we reached her bed. Debbe was unconscious.

*I*nner guidance sometimes comes as a nudge to go in a certain direction in which we are uncomfortable. It is always best to listen carefully and then decide for ourselves whether the guidance is reasonable and/or appropriate for us. But my inner guidance that day came with a sense of love so overpowering that I was not afraid. I did not hesitate to follow where it led.

As soon as I saw Debbe, I received a crystal-clear inner message about my sister. The voice said, "Touch her on her temple."

Brushing aside the nurse's protests, I quickly moved to my sister's side. The nurse took a step toward me as if intending to escort me from the area. Again, listening to my inner guidance, I turned and put my hand up, palm facing the nurse. She was not close enough for me to touch, but when I held up my hand, she moved backward.

There was an energy in this room that was far more potent than anything I understood, and the nurse seemed to feel it too. She no longer tried to remove me from the room; instead she explained more about Debbe's condition. But I couldn't listen fully. I had turned my attention to an urgent inner message: "Go to your sister.

Touch her on the temple, and hold your hand there. Then ask for the doctor immediately."

There were now two nurses present. As I followed the inner instructions that I was receiving, I turned and told them succinctly, "My sister needs me. Please get the doctor right away!"

Debbe was deathly pale, surrounded by machines and overlaid with tubes. I had never encountered a human being who looked so white, so lifeless. With Mom watching on, I went to the side of the bed.

Then I heard the words again: "Touch her temple."

My hand felt warm as I gently placed it on my sister's head again. I held it in place and felt the love between us. It is the love that unites us all, and when the love bond is strong, the link is real and tangible.

With my palm against her head, I moved my hand slightly this way or that, as I felt guided. I began to feel the terrible headache I had experienced the day before. It was so intense that I felt faint.

Then, I received another message: "Now shake both your hands repeatedly, and wash them well." There was a small sink in the room. I went over to it and shook my hands vigorously. Then I washed my hands thoroughly, as instructed.

The headache faded away like rapidly melting ice flowing down the drain. I quickly dried my hands and returned to my sister's bedside. Once again, I was told to put my hand on Debbe's temple, exactly like before, and I obeyed, tenderly touching her head.

To our amazement, Debbe slowly opened her eyes and spoke. "Annie, you're here," she acknowledged. "I had such an awful headache," she whispered.

"Is it gone?" I asked her.

"It's better now," Debbe acknowledged, smiling and

nodding her head ever so gently. "It was hurting so much."

This was an amazing experience. What had happened? I knew I had somehow been the vehicle for healing, but I didn't stop to think about that. I had just followed the inner direction from the Mahanta, and help had flowed through me.

"She's conscious. She's talking," I heard a nurse whisper animatedly as she entered the room.

I asked if the doctor was on the way. She nodded and looked anxiously out into the hallway.

My sister and mother spoke quietly to each other, and I kept my hand tenderly pressed against the side of Debbe's face. Then, unexpectedly, I was looking inwardly at an ethereal snapshot of the interior of my sister's brain. The gossamer image I observed existed somewhere between my sister's temple and my hand.

The area that needed attention was highlighted, like bold type in a medical manual. It caught my attention immediately, because it looked like something was definitely wrong. The inner guidance was coming in a visual way: There was something in her head that looked like a deflated balloon.

Dear God, how is this all happening? I wondered. But I only had a moment to think that. I knew my world was being rocked with spiritual experience upon spiritual experience—but I was even more aware that my sister's life was on the line.

It is sometimes this way when we take a big step in seeking truth and in our desire to know God. Our search for God does not remain esoteric; it comes into the core of our life. We're asked to serve in new ways, at deeper levels. As our search for God increases and our heart opens to the Holy Spirit, the spiritual Life Force increases. The spiritual inflow and guidance in our life often increase too, and in their wake comes change—change to a higher and greater level. It remedies those things that are out of harmony and allows the evolution of those things that are for our greatest good. And, yes, "everything is always happening exactly as it should, whether it appears that way or not."

Just then, the doctor arrived and quick introductions were made. Moving to Debbe's bedside, he greeted her kindly. He next spoke directly to me. "We don't know what is wrong with your sister. When she was brought into the hospital, she was unconscious. From what we understand, she was out with friends; she complained of a headache and then collapsed. One of her friends called for an ambulance, which rushed her here. She's been unconscious since, and her vital signs are very poor."

Mustering the courage, I told him about the inner image I had seen and the deflated balloon. Since I knew nothing about the anatomy of a brain, I asked if it were possible for there to be some sort of "deflated balloon" in Debbe's head.

"Yes, that's possible," he said. "If you have some idea of what's wrong, I'm listening." Then he asked eagerly, "Can you tell me exactly where the 'balloon' is and locate it on a drawing of the brain?" I nodded, and he gave me a sheet of paper with a bare outline of the two hemispheres of a brain.

The doctor's positive and enthusiastic response surprised me. No suspicion or doubt, just an attitude that clearly said, Let's get to work. I drew what I had seen, describing in detail the area surrounding the "balloon."

He listened intently, then said, "It could be an aneurysm—a stretched and weakened blood vessel which has ruptured. Possibly a ruptured cerebral aneurysm?"

Realizing he was actually posing the question to me, I listened inwardly for just a moment. The inner guidance was still strong. I confidently affirmed that my sister's condition was indeed an aneurysm. In this heightened state of awareness and inner guidance, I just knew. I didn't know how; I didn't care. I just trusted what I was feeling.

He asked me, "If I told you the names of several types of aneurysms, do you think you could help determine what kind it is?"

"Yes," I answered quickly before my mind could even begin to censor the reply. The doctor began to name various conditions, and when he spoke about hereditary aneurysms, I stopped him.

"That's it," I replied confidently. He nodded. This was apparently an important clue for him in piecing together my sister's current condition and how to approach it.

This was also illuminating information for me. A hereditary condition meant that Debbe had carried this condition all her life. I suddenly remembered a feeling I had as a child—that there was something physically wrong with my sister and that she needed help. Somehow, I had known. Even as a child, I had wanted to help my sister if I could, and often I asked God to use me for that purpose, if possible.

Had that time now come?

$\mathcal{O}$ne of my favorite passages in the writings of Eckankar explains just what I was experiencing at that moment. Harold Klemp writes:

> The ECK also works in ways of protection. It can come so quietly that we often overlook the message It carries: how to protect ourselves and

avoid unnecessary problems. We overlook the message because our state of consciousness hasn't quite expanded into the next circle of awareness. But when it does, we then get a bigger picture of life and a better idea of how the ECK is talking to us. When your inner feeling says, How about going left here a couple of steps, then right, then two more to the left, it's the ECK or the Mahanta trying to guide you through life. And because you are being guided by the spiritual power, you will be led in a better direction than the highest degree of reasoning could ever hope to steer you.[12]

My job was just to listen and follow the guidance. But it also occurred to me at that moment to ask the doctor why he was paying attention to what I said. It did not seem reasonable. Why would a surgeon from a top hospital be consulting with a young schoolteacher with no medical background?

In an urgent tone, he explained, "I've seen this before. You're having a spiritual experience. Right now you probably know more about what is going on than anyone else. In these circumstances, others sometimes know more than a doctor possibly could. If you believe there is an aneurysm located where you described it, I am prepared to operate. And hopefully your sister will live."

The doctor's conviction and acceptance helped me grow even more confident. I decided it was time to follow the fifth instruction I had received: "You must tell everyone concerned, 'This is not death.'"

"She will live," I told him. "She's not supposed to be dying."

Again the doctor nodded in confirmation of what I was telling him, and he smiled. He explained that operating was the only chance that my sister had to recover. My mom and I agreed to sign the papers allowing the doctor to perform the surgery immediately.

Debbe's operation took hours, but indeed the aneurysm was discovered. The doctor emerged afterward and told us that the surgery was a success and that the operation had gone smoothly. We were elated. Debbe was alive and well, and things had unfolded even better than the doctor had imagined.

Debbe was talking to us as soon as she came out of recovery. The doctor was very happy with her prognosis, and it was evident my sister was on the road to recovery. Soon, she could walk, talk, read, and write, and she seemed basically unimpaired. In fact, Debbe astounded everyone with her remarkable progress. Days passed, and her rapid recovery and healing continued, although she still had to spend several weeks in the hospital.

Soon after I returned home, however, a shocking incident occurred. During the night, Debbe woke up and stepped out of her hospital bed. She managed to walk down the empty hallway, stumble, fall, and hit her head.

The trauma caused a stroke, instantly paralyzing her on one side. The doctor believed the paralysis was caused by additional bleeding within the brain, which damaged adjacent, delicate brain tissue. As a result of the injury, Debbe could no longer walk properly, and her speech became slurred. She couldn't use her left arm or hand at all.

We were all deeply saddened. Everything had gone so extraordinarily well. Why this? Why had heaven and earth been moved to help Debbe, only to now have her facing such a demoralizing setback?

Yet, I remembered points number six and seven: "After this experience, this person will be better off than ever before. However, it will not appear to be so."

Was Debbe, in fact, better off than ever before, whether it appeared that way or not? I tried to understand what it was that my sister had to gain from this experience—what could possibly be to her spiritual advantage. I began to contemplate the challenges and the changes that this new development might bring to Debbe. What might the true blessings be? It was beyond my understanding.

The inner guidance I'd received was so very clear that I surrendered to its wisdom. I believed that somehow we would eventually see the blessings, despite the apparent difficulties Debbe was experiencing.

_D_ebbe's rehabilitation began after a short recovery time. She was scheduled to have physical, occupational, and speech therapy, which would continue for several months. There was a lengthy struggle to regain use of her left leg. She had the help of her therapists and doctors, but most of the work was solitary and difficult. Debbe grew in strength and determination.

In some ways, life had often been very easy for Debbe before this. She was popular, beautiful, and gifted in school—intellectually brilliant, passing every class with ease. She had easily found employment on Wall Street in New York's banking industry. Life had been Debbe's oyster.

Now, though, we could only stand by and watch, as Debbe made the Herculean effort required for her recovery. Through this time, she grew stronger in spirit. She was positive and did everything she needed for her fullest possible recovery. Her life was harder than it had ever been, yet now she was more open to God than ever before and saw miracles working in her life. One of the biggest gifts she received was through her own struggle.

She was learning patience, as well as compassion for others. I began to recognize that yes, Debbe was better off than ever before.

And this transformation gave her a special sweetness as another chapter unfolded in her life. During her struggle to learn to walk, drive, be independent, and return to work, suddenly she fell in love. Marty was good for her, treating her with consideration and kindness, and soon they were married. And, as time passed, Debbe gave birth to a son, Joey. She was, at that point, happier than I had ever seen her.

$\mathcal{A}$fter this experience with Debbe, I returned to my classes and my students and Jon. As I resumed my normal routine and moved with balance back into my career and friendships, the mystical experiences, the spiritual guidance, and the classroom drama continued to unfold.

Not surprisingly, my spiritual experiences only intensified. I had discovered how our inner guidance can protect us and those we love. It was beginning to dawn on me that such inner guidance is universally available to everyone—a gift from God—to help us learn to love more unconditionally. The time with Debbe highlighted what I was to learn more about later in Eckankar: there are solutions to our questions, issues, and problems that are beyond anything we can reason with our magnificent, yet not infinite minds.

And the most valuable lesson of all? It was number ten in my instructions, and it moved me to a new optimism and enthusiasm for life, born of faith and trust:

"Remember, everything is always happening exactly as it should, whether it appears that way or not."

9

Saying Yes to the Great Adventure of Life:

Inner Guidance Opens Amazing Doors

*Seize the moment, seize the day—and em-
brace life with joy and wonder. The ECK teachings offer you a simple way to enjoy life to the
fullest measure: the Spiritual Exercises of ECK.
Do them daily, do them well. For they bring love.*

—Harold Klemp
The Living Word, Book 2[13]

---

e were standing in the principal's office—
four teachers who all knew that one of us
was about to be asked to volunteer. "So who's
it going to be?" the principal demanded. No extra pay
and give up a Saturday. *Not a great idea,* I thought. He
was asking for a volunteer to escort a small group of top
students to a scholarship competition.

The test was over an hour's drive away, on a Saturday during summer vacation, which was about to
begin. *Nope, not me,* I inwardly responded as I turned
to step away.

Then I heard the still, quiet voice, more like a nudge than direct inner guidance. But it was there.

Oh, no! I was being *guided* to volunteer? Give up a whole day off for students I worked with all week?

Sometimes when we give to others, when we are willing to serve, we discover greater gifts waiting for us, more valuable than anything we might give. Whatever we give is returned to us many times over. We do not give for that reason, but it is a spiritual principle that is always working in our lives, whether we are aware of it or not.

Apparently, I was being guided to give.

Actually, I felt as if I were being pushed from behind—shoved, ever so gently—by the Inner Master. Could such a moment be worthy of the attention of the Mahanta, my inner guide? Yet, in truth, nothing is too minor for the Mahanta's loving attention.

Suddenly it did not matter that the test was being given in a remote school located in the Indiana countryside or that there was a long drive involved. Hesitating for only a moment, I sighed and spoke up.

"I'll do it," I replied quietly. I confirmed with the principal my willingness to take on this extracurricular mission.

In even the smallest things, as we learn to follow the lead of our inner guidance, we find the wisdom and gifts of the universe waiting for us.

When we arrived at the school, I was told that they had all the teachers they needed to help with the testing. The tests were to last four hours, so I was going to be free for most of the day, yet I was asked not to leave the campus.

The students and I had a bit of free time before

testing was to begin, so we explored the school. I quietly pondered my options as we checked out the place. The students asked me what I would be doing all day. The school library and classrooms were locked up tightly. I had not brought a book to read.

I started to express a regret—to say I wish I'd known and at least brought a book with me. Instead, I stopped myself and corrected my thoughts before they were expressed. I'd been talking with my students about the principle of expecting the best and selecting our thoughts wisely. This looked like a good time to make a conscious choice in the direction I was being guided—away from regret and toward trust and service, with a happy attitude.

Outside, through the windows, I saw tall, majestic trees surrounding the school property. Among them were wide paths stretching out in all directions. I would make the best of the time I had here and spend it relaxing and enjoying nature. I told the students I was delighted at the prospect of a long walk.

As we waited for the testing to begin, we saw a vending machine outside the cafeteria and descended upon it. I decided to buy a snack to take on my walk. There was the usual assortment of candy, with only one healthy exception: in the bottom row of the machine, there were plain brown bags of peanuts in the shell.

After depositing my coins and grabbing up a large bag of peanuts, I giggled and shared with the students the whimsical thought that popped into my mind.

"Now if only I had an elephant to share all these peanuts," I said, "life would be perfect!"

We all laughed.

I wished them well and watched as the students were ushered into the testing room.

Wandering outside into the fresh air and bright day, I took my treat to the back of the school. Several trails covered with natural wood chips lay before me. The widest pathway was off to the left.

As I turned to set off in that direction, my eyes grew wide in amazement.

There, not far from me, stood an elephant!

Looking all around, I saw no one else. This elephant could not be a school mascot, so why was it here? It was loose and just standing there. Someone responsible for this lovely animal had to be close by.

He was swaying gently under the trees, moving from foot to foot. As I looked at him, his trunk went up as if in a greeting.

I stood perfectly still for a moment or so, convincing myself this elephant was real. No reasonable explanations offered themselves. I looked in all directions; no one else was around. This elephant was just standing there, looking as if he were waiting for me.

Hadn't I just asked for an elephant to share my peanuts?

Our task, at all times, is to do all we can to stay in tune with our inner guidance. Yet sometimes it is amazing where Divine Spirit may lead.

At this stage in my spiritual growth, I was asking God to help me learn the spiritual laws—how the inner and outer laws of the universe worked via inner guidance. One particular spiritual law I was learning in Eckankar was the Law of Cause and Effect—how we manifest what we focus our attention on, positively or negatively. But this seemed far too direct and immediate to be a lesson in cause and effect. I was beginning to wonder if Divine Spirit or the Inner Master had quite a quirky sense of humor.

Yet the fact remained that I was standing on the

grounds of this rural Indiana campus, with a bag of peanuts in my hand, right in front of an elephant. When things occur that are quite out of the ordinary, there is always an important lesson. But what could be the lesson in stumbling upon an elephant on these school grounds?

Unversed in elephant etiquette, I very cautiously approached this enormous creature—a male elephant, an immense animal with feet the size of large buckets. Staying alert to any possible danger, I stepped a little closer.

The elephant stroked my face gently with his trunk. He was friendly!

I touched his body in response and felt his rough skin with its ridges and creases. He looked well cared-for and was in beautiful shape. He had clear, sparkling eyes and was grayish-black in color with a light dusting of dirt all over.

Overjoyed by the potential lessons inherent in this unusual encounter, I could not wait to tell the students. I was learning to keep my heart and mind open, to expect the best. I was also learning that we are never alone, and I sensed that in this very moment, the elephant and I were being carefully watched over by the Divine.

Expect the best; get it, and then some! But was there even more going on than that, more than just learning about cause and effect and the spiritual laws that govern all life?

I knew I was being carefully guided at all times; inner guidance had become second nature to me by this point in my life. So I was listening attentively to all the possible clues and inner messages that I knew were coming my way.

Yet, standing here with this elephant was outrageous. I imagined those in the heavenly worlds looking down at me with amusement, saying, "This will be fun to watch!"

It was a hot summer's day. I became concerned that the elephant might actually be lost, thirsty, and hungry. How long had he been here?

I asked the elephant to wait right where he was while I located a drink of water for him. Inside the school janitor's closet, I found a bucket. I rinsed it out, filled it with cool water, and headed back to the elephant. He drank with gusto. Then he looked at me, apparently asking for more. I repeated the process of fetching water, all the while congratulating myself. I had pleased the elephant and helped care for my new charge.

Then his trunk began to explore my pocket as if he were looking for something. Ah, the peanuts! I reached into the bag and took out a few. Now a new dilemma presented itself: How do you feed an elephant?

Holding the elephant's trunk in one hand, I carefully pushed a peanut gently into the opening at the end. I repeated this procedure with several other peanuts. I thought the elephant would then place the peanuts in his mouth and chew them.

I stood there, smiling in anticipation of the elephant's gratitude, but he was quick to let me know that my efforts at feeding him were misguided.

The elephant raised his trunk, pulled it back slightly, aimed at my face, and fired. A juicy peanut hit me on the forehead! My large friend was clearly offended by my ignorance of elephant peanut protocol. I'd received a quick lesson: do not stick peanuts up an elephant's nose.

"You didn't have to do that," I chastised. "I was only trying to help."

His trunk began to sway again around the pocket where the peanuts were stowed, so I bravely decided to try again. I took out the bag, opened it up, and offered all the contents to the elephant. He delicately took one peanut from the bag with his trunk, placed it in his mouth, and then reached for another. I began to offer the peanuts, one by one, on the open palm of my hand.

Ah, success! My elephant was happy once again.

Then I returned to the vending machine for several more bags of peanuts. I used up all my change buying lunch for the elephant and continued to feed him.

Next, I asked if he would like to join me for a walk. I turned to the path and set off into the woods. He seemed to understand me perfectly and began to saunter down the wide path, walking right beside me.

The elephant was about eight or nine feet tall at the shoulder. I was dwarfed next to him. For safety's sake, I leaned into him with my left shoulder as we moved along. He didn't mind the contact, and as I grew more relaxed with the situation, I rested my left arm comfortably against his leg. He lumbered along, swaying from side to side as we continued down the path.

I was experiencing something else as well. It was quite a surprise to me. The elephant seemed to have a very big heart, and it was filled with love which he was generously sharing with me. The love was so enormous, so all-encompassing, that I felt enveloped in it.

Everything about this adventure might have seemed fanciful, but I knew something much more was going on. I was being given a special gift of love—gentle, sweet, and huge all at the same time. I was brimming over with love and gratitude.

Suddenly, I felt strong inner guidance. I was being directed inwardly to speak to this elephant in pictures.

At first I wondered if this was just my imagination, but it seemed very clear. I had the sense that I should think in word pictures. I would imagine a picture and get another picture in return, and we two would communicate in quite an easy and natural way. It was extraordinarily effective.

I saw an inner image of a small circus tent. It wasn't a picture of my own making, so I sensed the elephant was telling me this was his home. The circus tent was where he needed to go, but I could not leave the school until the testing was over.

For now, we would just enjoy our walk together. We moved slowly along the path, and the elephant put his trunk around the back of my shoulders. I felt that he was expressing affection as his trunk gently and repeatedly caressed my cheek and the back of my neck. I was being embraced—freely given an enormous gift of affection and sweetness. I smiled and laughed as we walked and talked, and I felt bathed in the affection of this awesome creature.

It occurred to me that this beautiful meeting might never have happened if circumstances had not aligned perfectly. Had I refused the request to bring the students here, I would have missed this altogether. Had the library been open, I would have been there. Had I brought a book, I would have been reading. Had I been asked to be a proctor, I would have been sequestered with the students.

Grinning to myself while gently rubbing the elephant's neck, I marveled at the orchestration of the day's far-fetched events.

It was as if my inner guidance had softly pushed me through an opening in life's veil of illusion, and now suddenly the highly improbable was perfectly reasonable. As fantastic an adventure as it may have been—

walking for several hours through the tall woods, sharing peanuts with an elephant—it somehow seemed like the most natural thing in the world.

And my gift in all this was a moment in my life I will always treasure. Just by following the nudge to listen to my inner guidance and step up and volunteer, I received an enormous legacy of love.

$\mathcal{W}$hen it got close to the time the students' testing session would end, the elephant and I ambled back to the school. I reluctantly left my friend on the path and asked him to please wait for me.

Soon I found the students, who began to tell me about the difficult test. I listened to them for only a moment. Bursting with excitement of my own, I asked them to come to the back of the school because I had something to show them—a surprise. As we passed the vending machine, I teased them by saying that indeed the peanuts in the machine were for an elephant—the school mascot.

The students let me know they were not that gullible. No school had an elephant as a mascot.

They followed me outside, and I pointed immediately to my new companion. "Here he is," I announced, and I stretched to give him a big hug.

The students froze in their tracks. "Where did you get that elephant?" they demanded. "What's going on here?"

Rolling with laughter, I managed to tell them it was just a mysterious blessing from the universe. I really had no concrete answers. Guidance had opened me up to this experience. It was wonderful, wacky, wild, and fun—yet inner guidance, pure and simple.

This big, friendly fellow liked seeing the students

and waved his trunk gently to touch each one of them. They loved being acknowledged in this way.

Then I mentioned to them what I had seen inwardly as I "talked" with the elephant—a striped circus tent, probably in a nearby town—and I explained that I now needed to go and find it. Leaving the students with the elephant, I drove in search of his circus family.

The closest town was miles down the road. As I approached, I spotted the iconic striped circus tent with Ferris wheel and roller coaster—a small carnival, recently assembled. I parked and went around to the back, where there were large trucks and people milling about.

An aging, silver-haired man approached me. I asked, "Is this circus missing an elephant?"

He practically jumped at me! "Do you have him? You know where he is? I've been worried sick!"

When I saw how upset the man was, I quickly reassured him. "Yes, I found the elephant at a high school several miles down the road. We spent the day together," I admitted, "and he's with a group of my students now, having a good time."

I learned what a fine gentleman my elephant friend was and how he had never disappeared before. I couldn't help but be grateful that he had walked away from the circus this one time and visited me at the school.

*T*he elephant greeted his owner with great affection. Their reunion was emotional. It was clear this elephant had been given a lot of love. And although we had enjoyed only a short time together, he had certainly shared his love, touching my life and uplifting it.

When I returned to my school on Monday morning, the students had already shared the elephant story far and wide. Smiles greeted me as I walked through the hallways. People were touched by the mystery of the experience, the serendipity of it, that magical quality we all want to uncover in our own lives.

And in my heart, I now held the great love of an elephant—love easily shared, mysteriously given, and gratefully received.

Divine Spirit works in seemingly mysterious ways, and there are endless little blessings all around. And sometimes there are *really big* ones too!

Later, as I reflected on the events of that day, I saw new meaning in how inner guidance works in all aspects of our lives at all times. Our job is to stay open, listen to even the subtle nudges, and follow the directions of our heart. I was learning and growing, grateful for the love and guidance in every moment.

Inner guidance brought me to this very small act of service, and through service, it also gave me a huge gift. I expanded in my understanding of love through this simple experience.

We are all here to grow in love. Opportunities to blossom are all around us. As we love, serve others, and expect the best in all things, every day, Divine Spirit guides us very precisely to our greatest good. A simple but extraordinary approach to life, it is available to us all.

The gifts it brings are often life's greatest treasures.

10

Facing a Real and Present Danger:

Inner Guidance for Overcoming Fear

When you gain power over the fear of death, there is nothing that can hold you back in this life.

—Harold Klemp
The Book of ECK Parables, Volume 1[14]

When the shark appeared, I was well offshore, swimming freestyle, facedown. As I turned my head to take a breath, suddenly I was choked with fear. Far to my left, a dark fin moved directly toward me.

Adrenalin flooded my whole body, triggered by the basic instinct to fight or flee in the face of life-threatening danger.

Flight was not an option. I stopped swimming instantly. Stretching out my body, making it look as lean and long as I could, I attempted to float on the surface. I wanted to appear to be an inanimate object, just a bobbing mass on the ocean. I turned my head very slowly to the right, away from the approaching fin, so I'd be unable to watch the shark advancing toward me. I had nowhere to go, nothing to do except hold very, very still, stretched out like a log, with my arms tucked in by my sides.

But my heart would surely give me away. It was nearly pounding out of my chest, beating so rapidly, so hard, I could barely breathe. I closed my eyes and tried desperately to keep my mind from dwelling on the horror of being eaten by a shark.

It was Christmas vacation from school, and I was glad to be home to visit my mother and celebrate the holiday. Hilton Head Island is located off the coast of South Carolina. Natural pine forests bring shade to this environmentally protected island, and the oak trees are fringed with delicate, hanging Spanish moss. The crowning glory of this picturesque scene is a twelve-mile stretch of beautiful wide, sandy beaches.

On Christmas morning, Mom and I celebrated and opened gifts. Then I went to the beach alone and walked on the warm sands along the water's edge. It was a cool day, so although many people were walking and jogging on the beach, no one was swimming.

There were no lifeguards or caution flags. I longed just to dive into the ocean and swim. I would surrender to the ocean and be soothed by its vast strength. Always a strong swimmer, my family had once nicknamed me Fish because I taught myself to swim at the age of two.

But I stayed on the beach that morning, hesitant to face the chilly water. Around noon, though, I could resist no more, and I took the plunge, splashing my way into the deeper ocean waves, swimming hard and fast, feeling completely exhilarated.

I swam and swam, surrounded by the dark blue waters, until I rolled over on my back, exhausted and happy. Looking skyward, I took in the beauty of the mansion-sized clouds, then rolled over to look and see where I was relative to the shoreline.

Wow! I was so far from shore that the people walking the beach were suddenly very far away. How had I come out so far? It must have been a strong current that I failed to notice. With the force of a strong current, my every stroke had apparently taken me farther and farther into the ocean—much farther than my own efforts ever could.

Rip tides can drag you out to sea, where some people eventually drown if they struggle against them, trying to swim straight back to shore. The way to survive is to swim with it and gently edge out of it, until you swim parallel to the coastline and escape the seaward current. Only then can you swim back to land. I knew this; I'd grown up near the ocean.

The only other rule I learned as a child swimming these waters was Don't swim where the fishing boats are, since sharks trail them looking for easy food. Because it was Christmas day, there were no fishing boats around. Yet, I was out where the fishing boats would have been, and I could only hope the sharks wouldn't come looking for a meal.

Trying not to panic, I told myself that surely someone would notice me struggling to make my way back. Despite the distance from shore, I found some comfort in this possibility. I began swimming toward the coastline, prepared to rest when I needed a break. With so many people walking on the beach, I trusted that some sort of rescue mission would ensue if I couldn't make it on my own.

Then I saw the shark.

"Stay calm, stay calm!" I commanded my body.

In that heart-stopping moment, driven by an all-encompassing terror, I searched inwardly for what to do. I knew it was time for a serious talk with God. Quickly! I needed the hand of God to reach out of the sky and pluck me from this ocean.

Dear God, please . . .

Yes, we beseech God in times of trouble, and sometimes it is at those moments that we receive our greatest lessons and blessings.

Suddenly, inner guidance came. All my practice over the years of listening to the Divine came through. Although I was new to the teachings of Eckankar, I knew what to do. I would call upon the Mahanta, the Inner Master, for guidance and protection.

I had read in *ECKANKAR—The Key to Secret Worlds* that calling on this magnificent inner presence would bring the assistance of the Mahanta, the greatest spiritual guide in the heavenly realms. But could the Mahanta really escort me out of this life-threatening moment? Deliver me from a shark?

Being rescued is not always God's will, certainly. But if it was in this case, I wanted to use all that I knew to assist me. As the shark approached, I called out to the Mahanta again and again. Fine time for a test, but I had no choice.

Having delivered my plea, I stretched out like a log bobbing in the ocean. And though my heart was still racing outrageously, I experienced an immediate sense of emotional relief. A moment of absolute surrender passed through me like a gentle wave.

I felt almost invisible in the water. No longer gripped

by the paralyzing fear, I faced death with calmness, floating in one eternal moment of peace.

Suddenly, I was hit hard from underneath.

The impact was powerful, and my body jolted up out of the water and shot forward like a bullet. Was this an attack? The force of the blow was bone-jarring, yet I felt no pain.

And then the most amazing thing happened. For the briefest moment, I was suspended in the air, above the water. Then I felt my body falling back into the ocean. I was hit again.

I didn't understand what was happening, and my heart continued to pound wildly, yet still I felt no pain.

I felt the strange hitting sensation slam against me a third time. Then a powerful, smooth, sleek body approached from my right side, and suddenly rose up underneath me, lifting me right out of the water!

I was rapidly moving across the surface of the ocean, speeding toward the shore.

The surface of the water broke in front of me, and I saw the heaven-sent rescuer on whose back I had just been carried. It was a beautiful dolphin, piercing the waves and jumping through the air in the inimitable way of these intelligent mammals. Just then another dolphin lifted me. Poised on the back of this second dolphin, I was again speeding through the water effortlessly. A third dolphin looked right at me as it dived to the left and submerged.

A school of dolphins had come to my rescue! They surrounded me, carrying me away from the shark!

It was beyond belief, yet I struggled to pay attention and stay aware. I wanted to remember every moment of it forever. I wanted to capture every detail of this thrilling experience as the dolphins took turns lifting me, turning me into a human hydroplane.

As these graceful creatures swam from underneath me, each one would leap and splash ahead of the group, dancing a magnificent high-speed ballet. My movement through the water seemed surreal; it was part floating, part soaring, and part balancing act. Yet, I did nothing. With total control of my body, the dolphins made all the necessary adjustments to keep me flying effortlessly through the water.

Quickly and smoothly, they brought me to the safety of chest-deep water near the beach. As I breathlessly turned to take in what was happening, I saw I was standing upright in the ocean, surrounded by an entire school of Atlantic bottlenose dolphins.

They continued to encircle me, spinning, diving, and smiling. Pirouetting on their tails, they performed their extraordinary dance. They were in no hurry to leave. They called out in a wonderful, high-pitched language that spoke to my whole being. They were communicating all the joy and beauty of the moment in a graceful, gorgeous concert. Synchronistic flying, twirling, and leaping combined with a harmony of other-worldly voices!

"Dear God, thank you, thank you," I cried as gratitude filled my whole being. "Thank you, Mahanta!"

Watching the dolphins, I felt this was truly their celebration for my safe return to shore. A job well done! Surrounded by the entire group, I clapped with glee and cried out my praise and appreciation for both my rescue and their splendid performance. I spun round and round, talking to them out loud, thanking them all for this marvelous blessing.

Whatever they were communicating, the message was clearly of love and pure joy. Touched and in awe, I responded with euphoric cries in return, "I love you! Thank you! Thank you. Yes! Yes! I love you too!"

Eventually, the dolphins turned and danced backward for several feet in a perfect farewell. I watched as they formed two lines and skipped and splashed their way out to sea in a thrilling, choreographed ballet.

"*D*o you work with dolphins?" an excited onlooker called out.

A crowd of people had gathered on the beach and waited to greet me, laughing and talking excitedly. They questioned me about the dolphins, wondering if I was a trainer who worked with them.

I laughed and shook my head. "No, I've never even seen the dolphins around this island before." Tears of joy and relief glistened in my eyes. "I think they came to save me from the current. I was carried so far out into the ocean."

That's what I wanted to believe. There was no shark, I told myself, relieved. It was dolphins, dolphins all along.

An old man stepped out of the crowd at that moment. "Those dolphins saved your life," he stated soberly. "I saw that shark coming for you." He nodded his head in solemn certainty. "It was coming right at you. Those dolphins knew you needed help, and they rescued you."

*T*he old man was right. Nodding affirmation, I admitted that I also knew it was true about the shark. Were dolphins sent to my rescue?

I had followed my inner guidance and called out to God, asking for help from the Mahanta. I wasn't sure how it all worked from a spiritual point of view, but my plea was heard. Of that I was certain.

It was clear that there was a power in the universe beyond anything I had ever conceived—a power that could pull together all the forces of nature in a split second to change the course of events in our lives.

And today that awesome power had saved my life.

The experience left me with a strong sense of the interconnection of all life—and an awareness that God's love, guidance, and protection are always with us. It does not matter how isolated we might feel; we are never alone.

After that experience, I was a changed person—as anyone might be. I took all that love and brought it back to my life, my career, and my relationships.

And I learned a depth of trust that permeated everything I did from that day forth.

11

Breaking through the Hard Human Shell:

Inner Guidance Brings a New State of Awareness

Light and Sound, just like the rain and the wind, come to everyone equally and alike. But some people benefit more than others.

It's up to you in your state of consciousness.

And your state of consciousness depends upon whether or not you care enough to open yourself to this inner guidance of Divine Spirit so that you can have some of the experiences that are necessary to break through this hard human shell. Unless you do, you cannot rise into the higher states of awareness.

—Harold Klemp
How to Survive Spiritually in Our Times[15]

I was at a crossroads, and I did not even know it. It was such a simple thing, but the consequences were enormous.

Since I had begun my study of Eckankar, I had

107

received monthly lessons called ECK discourses. I read one per month, reviewing and discussing it in a class called a Satsang. I really liked Satsang. In this sharing, my awareness and understanding became more refined. I found new insights into my own life even as I sat and listened to others.

In Satsang, students of ECK find encouragement and regularly receive their own inner guidance, particularly into the meaning of the text as it relates to their own lives. Or they might find answers to one or more of the issues they may be facing. In my own experience, the tangible presence of the Mahanta was with us in the class.

Participating in Satsang was often a highlight of the month. I looked forward to getting together with the class to study the truth and wisdom found in the discourses.

Yet, time was at such a premium in my life; I needed more of it. I was married and very busy at the university, working for five professors and expanding my own studies in education. Attending Satsang class was sometimes hard to work into my schedule, and it got to where I felt I could get by just reading the ECK books and studying on my own.

The decision to follow the path of Eckankar is always left to the individual; it is personal and private. Only you can decide what meaning and purpose the teachings have and how they fit into your life. So it seemed a reasonable approach to my spiritual study to just take a breather—a little break.

Quitting Satsang and not renewing my membership in Eckankar and its study program was a decision I made perhaps a bit too lightly. I intended to reread my ECK discourses on my own, and mostly I felt fine about my decision, yet some part of me was a little hesitant, a little saddened.

But on a practical level it seemed like a good decision. After all, my life was so busy. It would free up much needed time and energy.

*S*urprisingly, life began to change all at once. Very abruptly, it lost its glow.

Perhaps this is not always the case, but for me, there was no doubt. Life was on a downhill spiral in every arena. I was suddenly having trouble keeping up with my work. I felt exhausted. Everyone seemed more demanding. My days became more stressful and frustrating.

My classes at the university were no longer going well either. A big grant that would have funded my work with the university was being reassessed, and my salary was cut. Unexpectedly, my prospects were not looking good. Worse yet, an important program that I had applied for with the university was canceled. I was disheartened.

A general malaise was coming over me, and I did not like it. How could all of this have happened in such a short period?

What had happened? Only a short time ago, my life seemed so charmed, so exciting.

At first, I did not link the changes in my life with my change of heart regarding Eckankar and my commitment to spiritual study. I only wondered if there was something I could do, inwardly or outwardly, to escape this difficult place I found myself in and bring things back to their formerly wonderful state.

Eckankar had introduced me to a simple spiritual exercise, singing HU. By now, I was quite accustomed to singing HU daily as an unconditional song of love to God. Often I focused on love or God during my daily spiritual exercise; now I decided that it would be best to contemplate deeply on my life and see if I could find any insights or clarity. I simply surrendered all the issues to Divine Spirit and asked for guidance.

So one morning before work, I sat with my eyes closed and sang HU several times: "HU-U-U-U, HU-U-U-U, HU-U-U-U." I took a deep breath and, following an inner nudge, stopped chanting and sat quietly in contemplation. Then I began to chant again: "HU-U-U-U, HU-U-U-U, HU-U-U-U." I could feel the Sound Current, the Voice of God, filling me and flowing through me, like a wave of love washing away the problems of the day.

All of a sudden, clear inner guidance flooded my consciousness.

There *was* a time when all these changes had begun!

In a flash I could see when that was. It started with my decision to stop receiving the ECK discourses and to no longer be in Satsang. Eckankar classes and my Eckankar membership—could something so simple be so important?

In my inner vision, I could see it clearly: I had stepped off the fast track and onto a long, slow, dreary road where life was much more difficult and demanding. Previously I had felt like an electric lamp burning brightly. Now I felt unplugged, with no energy in my life to help illuminate me and give the spark that once brought such high motivation and vitality.

How could Eckankar membership really matter *so* much? I still loved the teachings, still sang the HU.

Taking a moment, I considered what it represented. My Eckankar membership seemed to correspond to a commitment to the Divine. I had simply changed my level of commitment, and my spiritual linkup had changed accordingly.

Eckankar is said to be a direct path to God. I definitely felt the presence of God more strongly than ever once Eckankar came into my life. When I made my initial decision to study the teachings, I sensed that I had connected with a source of great, momentous energy. Outstanding synchronicity marked my days.

But at the moment, that was gone. Instead, I now saw an image that I did not like: The flow of life, like a great river, had been diverted, and I was left in a barren land. By my own choice, I had cut myself off from that current. Standing out in a desert—hot, dry, and deserted—I was alone. How others might live like this, I did not know, but I could hardly bear it.

I had to do something about this at once.

$\mathcal{I}$ wrote a small donation check to Eckankar and enclosed it with a request to renew my membership and resume my study of the ECK discourses. I made a phone call to arrange to join a new Satsang. These were minor, outer things to do, but it felt like a significant inner commitment.

This will be an experiment, I decided. As long as I am still receiving the many benefits I have experienced from this spiritual study—the energy, love, insights, and guidance—I will continue as a member of Eckankar and give it my all.

That was the commitment I made to myself that day.

I took the envelope with my membership renewal request down to the post office and, with a sense of relief, dropped it in the mailbox.

$\mathcal{W}$hen I returned home that afternoon, the phone was ringing. To my great delight, I learned that the project at the university was back on. A meeting had just ended; my name had come up, and it had been determined that I was to be part of an important study of education in the United States.

In fact, I had been selected to be in charge of my component of the study. Could I come to meet with the committee tomorrow?

This was a dream come true. Life was back on track! I would have about two weeks to prepare, and then I'd be off on an exciting adventure, documenting alternative approaches to high-school education in a five-state area.

Although I didn't know it at the time, that trip would result in an important job offer and opportunities that would put my career in high gear. I would remain out west and work with the public schools on innovative programs.

The message was obvious. Because I had made this spiritual commitment, new doors opened and brought an increased flow of Spirit into my life. I had realigned myself with Divine Spirit's all-loving guidance. The choice had been mine.

I marvel at the opportunities we are given for greater awareness—opportunities to look at our lives and use our experiences as a gauge for spiritual progress.

I've continued in Satsang ever since, studying uninterruptedly year after year. And I've found I am always satisfied, always gaining more and more. The benefits are undeniable. I feel more peace, more love, more joy, and a constantly growing connection with the Divine.

Our inner guidance, the clear channel to God's gentle voice, always knows the way to help us move into a new and higher state of consciousness. The guidance is always there, if only we ask and listen for the unique ways God speaks to us.

Life was about to give me another gift, completely unexpected although definitely previewed by inner guidance. It would show me how abundant the blessings of God are for all of us, at all times.

12

The Gift Has Already Been Given:

Inner Guidance to Accept Our Abundant Blessings

We must know that the gift is made even before we see it. Consciousness must receive the gift before it comes into manifestation on this physical plane.

—Paul Twitchell
The Flute of God[16]

The communication began, "You will teach for ten years . . ."

I waited to hear about the wonderful things that would happen to me during those ten years! But the message continued in a completely different vein, in a direction that caused me confusion and some concern: "and then you will teach no longer."

At times, we may not like the inner guidance we receive, but as we recognize the truth it brings, we can learn to trust it and ourselves. Our guidance should prove itself over time as our lives unfold. Guidance is not always crystal clear, nor is it something we follow blindly. Yet occasionally, incredibly lucid inner messages do come through. In those moments, it is obvious that Divine Spirit is answering a question or telling us something important.

So, like it or not, I knew I had to pay attention. I have to admit, I was taken aback. Ten years! Before receiving this message, I felt absolutely certain that teaching would be my lifelong career. I could not imagine anything I'd rather do than teach high school. And what would cause me to stop teaching after ten years? I did not care at all to embrace this message.

I made an effort to calm myself. Perhaps this was only a *symbolic* message, like the one about having a baby. Besides, ten years was a long time. Still, I loved teaching! I was gaining national recognition for programs I was implementing, and my students were winning acclaim for their achievements.

Typically, when going into contemplation, I began my inner conversations by chatting happily, with no intention of being demanding or impertinent. Contemplation was a time for trying to quietly discover how to strengthen my relationship with the Divine. But this time I was uncertain how to proceed. Bumbling along and trusting that any errors I made would be tolerated, I now begged for clarity.

"But why?" I pleaded silently.

My questions were endless. Were all my plans and dreams to be suddenly turned to dust? After ten years, I would simply leave teaching completely? Would I not have a chance to reconsider the wisdom of this decision? Would something happen that would cause me to *want* to make such a change?

Then I heard the message repeated very clearly. "You will teach for ten years, and then you will teach no longer."

My inner guidance had shown me long ago that Divine Spirit was tolerant, at least to a certain extent. In turn, I was willing to trust in this guidance and consider that whatever the outcome, it would be for my greatest good. Teaching was my passion, however, and I told myself that I would stay right where I was as long as it remained for the greatest good of my students and me.

I whispered inwardly, "I release all my concerns to Divine Spirit." I would continue teaching—with confidence and love. Yet, if there were something even greater than this, I wanted to remain open to it, to experience the fullness of my life. I surrendered my concerns by simply saying, "If not this, then something greater!"

$\mathcal{I}$t was a time of change and growth. I was learning to do the Spiritual Exercises of ECK faithfully to stay in tune with the wonderful inner help and guidance that is always there. My commitment to the teachings of ECK was strong.

And my outer life was reflecting the abundance of my inner spiritual life.

I wanted career help, as I sought to move into the higher echelons of secondary alternative education. I was grateful for the invitation from Indiana University to go out west and supervise an educational project. Once there, true to my guidance, I was offered a position, and I felt the gentle inner nudge to say yes and stay.

It would be months before my husband, Jon, could join me in Utah. He was a builder, and he had just contracted to build a house back in Indiana. I was getting used to my new teaching and administrative position, and there were plenty of things to occupy my time. I was enjoying the new challenges.

The friends with whom I was temporarily staying were expecting a baby. I watched the process of preparing for the birth and attended educational sessions with my friend and her midwife. In Utah, natural childbirth was encouraged and considered the most desirable choice. By sharing this process with my friend, I began to connect deeply with the concept of being a mother and to vicariously experience this special aspect of being a woman.

During that time of change, my dreams became exceptionally vivid. They included a series of visions that revealed how profoundly I wanted a baby. I remembered the message that had come through, loud and clear, as I sat at that stoplight back in Indiana not so long ago.

The timing seemed terrible, and the likelihood poor, but the longing was earnest and inescapable.

Susanna's baby arrived. I assisted with the birthing process. Even though the delivery took many hours, it was a wonderful experience. Baby Bart could not have been more precious, and the midwife was remarkable. I appreciated every moment.

Holding the baby right after he was born, I cried tears of both joy and sorrow. The feelings I was having were almost unbearable. I had to leave the house and go for a walk. Meandering through the woods, I wept in longing for the baby that the doctors had told me I could never have. As I cried, I questioned whether there could have been any truth to that inner message I had heard while waiting in my car for the light to change: "You will have a child before you are thirty, and it will change your life."

Time was short then; now there was even less time left. But I was married, so one obstacle was overcome.

Surrounded by rugged mountains, I inhaled deeply of air filled with the clean smell of pine. The weather was crisp as I paused in a secluded spot in the fading sunlight. Through sobs, I spoke aloud to God and the universe: "I want a baby. If I *agreed* never to have a child in this lifetime, I have definitely changed my mind. I want a baby!"

I stamped my foot just to seal the deal.

Frustration with my choices had prompted this outburst. I had come to understand that before birth in each lifetime, we participate in a sort of planning process in the spiritual worlds. There are certain lessons due us. We foresee many of the experiences we will have and the people with whom we will have them. This becomes our probable destiny. Yet, as I understood it, the Mahanta, the Living ECK Master could help us to go beyond that probability and fulfill our greatest possible achievements on every level.

Perhaps regretfully, sometime after we are born, most of us suffer varying degrees of amnesia about the whole planning process. Nevertheless, I knew I could rely on the guidance and protection of the Mahanta as I made it known that I wanted to change the plan.

Yet, I wondered if that were even possible.

$\mathscr{E}$verything seemed to hinge on this moment. I felt a softening in my heart as I spoke to the Mahanta, the Inner Master. "I want to have this experience. Please," I pleaded. "I want it! I want to change the plan for my life, and I want a baby."

We should always want God's will to be expressed in our lives, and I felt deeply connected with the divine will in this desire. Still, I was not beyond begging, just in case it might help me in some way with this manifestation in my life.

Standing in the woods that day, I ached deeply with

the desire to have a baby, and the Mahanta surely knew what was in my heart. As if in reassurance, I again thought of my previous inner message: "You will have a child before you are thirty, and it will change your life." That was what I heard. Yet, how could it be true?

Surrender finally came—meltingly, softly, gently inside. I whispered, "Thy will be done."

Then, adding my beloved statement of surrender that seemed to take it all to an even higher level, I smiled and said, "If not this, then something even greater."

Maybe I had not fully comprehended the meaning of the inner message or been able to believe it, but the promise now seemed real, and somewhere deep inside I suddenly caught a glimpse of what it meant: I was *supposed* to have a baby! That was why I was having this revelation.

The facts, however, weren't promising. I would turn twenty-nine in spring. And sadly, I had to concede that my marriage to Jon was in trouble.

Regardless, the fervent desire for a baby persisted. I released all pain and doubt, yet I gently continued to cry until I could cry no more.

$\mathcal{I}$n my study of Eckankar, I had learned about the Blue Light.

"Those of you in Eckankar are very familiar with the Blue Light," Harold Klemp writes. "This is a sign of the Holy Spirit, the Sound and Light of God speaking to the individual. Sometimes It comes as Light and sometimes It comes as Sound. Sometimes It comes as both."[17]

As I stood there in that secluded, wooded spot, I felt a response. The Sound Current seemed to answer in the wind in the trees. Was it the ECK, the Audible Life Stream, that I heard, swirling and calling all around me?

What was the sound buzzing in my head? And this high-pitched call that pierced through my cries?

Ah, yes, it was the Voice of God, which can be heard as Sound and seen as Light. I had already experienced It in the inner worlds, as the Light and Sound of God, yet now It palpably permeated the outer world in which I stood.

As the Sound became louder and louder, I saw the Light inwardly—blue, blue everywhere.

"Help me, please," I spoke aloud to the trees, the sky, and the ground where I stood. My tears had stopped, yet I admitted to the Mahanta and all who would listen, "I want my child. I want the inner message to be true and real. I want the child I am promised."

Then I dropped to my knees in reverence and exhaustion.

*W*ith the festivities of the holiday season and the New Year, the next two months passed quickly. I had been in Utah for just over six months when Jon arrived in town, and we moved into a house together. I was very busy with teaching, and Jon went to work immediately, helping to build a large house for a new client.

Our relationship seemed to be a little better than it had been previously, in Indiana, but things were still tentative. Despite my personal longing, the timing did not seem right to talk about having children.

I took on new responsibilities at work, as my alternative high-school programs were growing. One curriculum was environmentally based, and we did a lot of outdoor activities. Once snow began to fall, the students and I skied several times a week up to the top of a local mountain to take samples of snow, water, and other natural elements for study at the university.

One day, at a particularly high elevation, the world began to spin; I became lightheaded and incredibly ill. I felt so faint and disoriented that it would have been dangerous for me to try to ski. So the students practiced their rescue skills; using my skis as a sled, they slid me down the slopes, flat on my back. They managed nicely, and as soon as we were off the mountain, I felt fine.

Just to be certain, however, I went straight to a doctor.

The tests I took at the clinic came back quickly, and the results were mind-boggling. The doctor sat opposite me at his big mahogany desk. Coolly and kindly, he explained with a smile, "Well, my dear, all of our concerns were for nothing. The fact of the matter is, you are pregnant!"

In an automatic response, my arm swept across his desk, knocking down anything that stood in the way of a perfectly clear line of communication. Pens, books, and papers all scattered and fell to the thick carpet. The doctor looked at the mess and laughed.

"I take it this is a surprise?" he asked with a twinkle in his eye.

"Why do you think I am pregnant? What's that got to do with dizziness and feeling faint?"

"Your hormones are quite elevated—sky high, as is typical for the first trimester—and you couldn't handle the altitude, I suspect. That happens sometimes. When was your last period, exactly?"

"I don't have any usually," I said. "Not any normal ones. I've been told I can never get pregnant. And if I am pregnant, this is *not* my first trimester."

"That's confusing. Well, it would be hard to tell without further tests, but since you don't look . . ." he began.

Interrupting to help him better understand the situation, I added, "I don't know about the tests, but if I am more than just a few *days* pregnant, I am at least six *months* pregnant. My husband has been more than fifteen hundred miles away for over six months. Until he arrived a week ago, I had no chance of getting pregnant."

He looked at me, shook his head, and unscientifically remarked, "You don't look six months pregnant; you're far too thin."

I skied often and hard. Also, in the environmental program I taught, my students and I had recently taken up rock climbing. I peered down at my flat, toned stomach and asked the doctor, "How could I be sitting here six months pregnant?"

"Well, this is confusing," he repeated. "No, you definitely don't look six months pregnant; certainly not. Do you think there could be some mistake?"

"None. Six months or nothing," I responded firmly.

"We will have to take further tests, then. I must tell you that with the hormone levels you are showing, if you are not pregnant, it could be something else very serious," he warned.

We took the tests, and I went home.

Exhausted and confused, I needed to relax and take a long, hot bath. Could it be true? Was I to have a child before I was thirty? Would the prophecy be real? As my mind whirled with the thoughts of the last few hours, I fell asleep in the tub of warm water.

When I awoke, I called the midwife my friend Susanna had used to assist with birthing baby Bart. I asked if she could come and examine me just to see if, in fact, I might actually be pregnant.

She said she could come in a half hour, so I dressed

and waited nervously for her arrival.

I hadn't mentioned how far along I might be, but Rhona took only a few minutes to size up the situation. She touched my stomach area, felt around under my chest, examined my body for a few moments more, and then confirmed, "You're almost full-term. I would say about six and a half months, maybe a little more. If you want me to help you in a natural childbirth, you need to put on a lot of weight to support this pregnancy."

Bingo! She said the magic words—six months or more. Jon and I looked at each other in amazement. That was precisely how long we had been apart.

"But if I am that far along in this pregnancy, why is my stomach so totally flat?" I asked incredulously. "How could this be? Is the baby OK?"

"My guess," she said, "is that your baby is lying laterally from hip to hip—lodged in tightly in that position. And you have been exercising a lot and not eating enough. If we turn the baby now, while it's still so small, you should both be just fine." While she explained this, she began to open her bag and pull out a sterile sheet and gloves.

A short time later, Rhona confirmed the presence of a new life inside me. And she had turned the baby in the right direction. Like magic, my stomach began to swell and swell and swell—like something out of a science-fiction movie! I went from a flat stomach to the look of an almost full-term pregnancy in less than a half hour. We all laughed at the sight.

"What about morning sickness and all that?" I asked the midwife. "I never felt *anything* like that at all. I felt great until my last ski trip."

"It's different for every woman. Some women don't get sick; they feel better than ever when they are pregnant. Apparently that is how your body is functioning.

That's how it is for some women," she explained casually.

A powerful realization struck me. Only a short time ago, while I had been crying for a baby, after Susanna's birthing, my baby was already growing strong inside me. There I had been, pleading, begging, and demanding from God what I wanted, and I was already very pregnant—with the child I had been told I could never have.

Before I had even known my own heart, before I had even thought to ask—the gift had already been given!

My thoughts raced wildly. *The gift had already been given!*

I was begging and pleading for something I already had? Is it always that way? Is what we desperately want already waiting for us—somehow, some way? Do we truly have to just step up and accept the gift? Could it be that simple?

What I knew for sure was what was true for me. The gift had already been given—and an important spiritual lesson was received as well. Now I understood it for myself.

And inner guidance had proved true again, even though it sounded impossible at the time.

13

Learning about Inner Masters:
Inner Guidance and Inner Realities

Each of us is a unique individual, with our own peculiar combination of experiences accumulated over many lifetimes. The truth of ECK comes to each of us like a special key, custom-designed with millions of little notches and grooves. It is the only key that will fit the lock, turn it, and open the door of Soul.

—Harold Klemp
Unlocking the Puzzle Box[18]

*O*ur inner guidance is custom-made for each of us, and it can help us create perfect solutions for ourselves spiritually and in every detail of our lives. We each understand things uniquely, desire different things, and have different experiences. So our answers come uniquely as well. Our inner guidance perfectly responds to our needs, desires, challenges, questions, and state of consciousness at any given time.

When I first came into Eckankar, I wondered about

the ECK Masters. The Eckankar writings spoke of these amazing beings. Were they truly real? And could they work with me through inner guidance, in the dream state, and in my waking life? Would this have any outer effect in my life?

Before finding Eckankar, I had often felt alone and separated from God. I wanted to know I was loved and was part of some wonderful, mysterious plan of the Divine for my spiritual growth.

So one evening, I sat on my bed and sang HU. I imagined myself walking with one of the ECK Masters. As I did this, I felt better inside. Nothing big happened at first, but my inner guidance nudged me to focus on a scene like this each night before bed. *What a good idea,* I thought.

Thus my spiritual experiment with the ECK Masters began.

Each night, as I sang HU, this holy name for God, I pictured myself walking with an ECK Master. At the time I had been reading *ECKANKAR—The Key to Secret Worlds* by Paul Twitchell, the modern-day founder of Eckankar, so I chose him as my ECK Master to walk with. I asked him inwardly for guidance during the dream state and for insights into the questions I had about the nature of life and why I was here.

Nights passed without any special visitations. But I didn't give up. My inner guidance said to persist until something happened.

*T*here are many ECK Masters written about in the Eckankar teachings. The spiritual leader of Eckankar, Harold Klemp, often appears to students of Eckankar in his inner form, as the Mahanta, the Inner Master. He is known on the inner planes as Wah Z. Anyone can sing

HU or the name Wah Z before sleep (or anytime) to invite the Mahanta. The Mahanta and all the ECK Masters are watching over us much more than we might imagine. And they are all part of an ancient line of spiritual guides or Masters, the Order of the Vairagi.

One of the most beloved distinguishing hallmarks of these Vairagi ECK Masters is their deep observance of the Law of Love. They allow each Soul total freedom to invite their help—or not. Only when invited will they provide specific assistance or guidance.

As Harold Klemp writes, "The ECK Masters never interfere in another person's state of consciousness without his permission. I hold your personal life sacred and won't intrude in any way, even in the dream state, without your permission."[19]

So each night, I gave permission. I asked sincerely for spiritual assistance in knowing myself better as Soul.

At first, when the different ECK Masters began to appear in my dreams to address my questions, I could recognize them only by the light around them. I knew they must be ECK Masters because of the glowing brilliance and the accompanying sense of love and tranquillity that their presence radiated. Yet I still believed, as many people do, that these visits were somehow only a product of my imagination.

One night in the dream state, all of this changed. I could see an ECK Master walking toward me, still quite a distance away from me, and a swirl of questions began to rise within me.

"Are you a figment of my imagination?" I silently asked this being. "I am not sure who you are supposed to be, but I am sure I have somehow created you. Maybe this whole dream is just my imagination and you are just a part of it."

The ECK Master continued walking in my direction, not responding. I studied him. I could feel the light and love emanating from him—my signal that he was indeed an ECK Master. But I had not even done a very good job of picturing him. He was bald! Surely ECK Masters should have hair.

So as he approached slowly, I tried to imagine hair on his head. Long blond locks? No, that wasn't it. Short-cropped black hair? Somehow that didn't feel right either. I made several more attempts to adorn this Master with an imaginary hairstyle, but none worked well at all.

I was wondering what to attempt next, when he drew closer and spoke.

"Anne," this bald ECK Master declared clearly and firmly, "I'm real."

"You're real?" I asked. "But isn't this a dream? Aren't you just a character in my dream—in my imagination?"

"This is the dream state," he said gently, "but I'm as real as you are."

"You are?"

"Why wouldn't I be? You're here, and *you* are real."

I loved that. Yes, I was real, and I was in this dream too. His explanation was more clever than anything I would have thought of myself. I studied him more closely.

He laughed aloud, not at all rattled by my neophyte behavior. By this time, he was standing right next to me. "I'm real, *and* I'm bald!" he playfully announced.

We both laughed.

My imagination had not *created* this man any more than it had created me. Imagination is only the genesis of the process of opening the door to greater realities. This was an actual being, fully formed and real, apparently here to visit with me.

I'd learned this important truth by following my inner

guidance, persisting with my nightly spiritual exercise. This experience took me another step toward greater acceptance and appreciation of the ECK Masters.

*T*his ECK Master and I walked along together. He talked to me quite easily. He explained how Soul comes into the lower worlds, the worlds of time and space, where duality reigns. Untried and yet fully capable, Souls descend into the worlds below for experience—to gain confidence and discover their true nature.

"What is *true nature*?" I asked.

"Look at this," he said.

He opened an extremely large pocket on the side of his robe. Taking a quick peek inside, I saw what looked like innumerable twinkling stars. He took some out and held them in the palm of his hand.

"What do you see?" he questioned as I peered at the tiny specks of dazzling light.

I looked closely, yet at first I saw only extremely small stars, radiating a breathtaking luminescence. I described to him what I saw.

"Look more closely," he urged. "Tell me, what do you see now?" He held up his hand so I could take a better look.

By now, I was completely in this inner experience, which was very real, as real as my everyday life. In Eckankar, the Mahanta teaches Soul to become more and more comfortable with these inner planes, the places where we can each go to learn more about ourselves as spiritual beings.

I examined the ECK Master's palm, closely inspecting the ever-so-tiny stars. But as I peered at them, suddenly I saw that the tiny stars were not stars at all! "They're alive!" I exclaimed. "They are little living beings!" They appeared to be illuminated by their own internal flame.

"They're new Souls—pure, individual sparks of the Light and Sound of God," he whispered sweetly as he tossed them gently into a dark, vast sky. They tumbled lightly and slowly, like weightless, glowing, downy seeds carried by a soft breeze. "They are love—unique beings of divine love," he declared with reverence.

Marveling at their beauty, I watched them slowly cascading down. There was no sense of shame or failure as is often associated with the fallen status of human beings in this earth world. This ECK Master spoke of these Souls with the highest regard and tender affection. I came to know this as a common trait among all ECK Masters—this reverence for all life. These Souls were gloriously sailing to their great adventures, ready for the immense world of experience with all its opportunities, tests, and trials.

He explained to me that they would make it, each in Its own way, to full awareness of their unique beauty, gifts, and purpose. Each would become a Co-worker with God, loving and serving all life unconditionally.

I understood that he meant me too.

When I awoke, I could still hear his voice. I had never seen him before, but I distinctly remembered what he looked like and hoped that I might learn who he was. If he were truly real, as he had told me, could I find out more about him?

He had mentioned his name, but I did not remember it when I awoke. It reminded me of the word *bubble*, but that certainly was not what he said.

There was an Eckankar center near my home, so I went there the next day. I wanted to see if I could find a picture of this ECK Master. My question was quickly answered by the volunteer at the reception desk.

He showed me some drawings of ECK Masters, and there he was: my ECK Master, bald and magnificent. His name was Yaubl Sacabi. I had never seen his picture before, but I recognized him instantly. There was no doubt it was the ECK Master who had simply, yet clearly, shared so much wisdom and love in my dream.

After this inner meeting with Yaubl Sacabi, I moved into a new and greater level of trust and acceptance of the reality of the ECK Masters. Despite my previous doubts, my call for guidance had been heard.

When we follow our unique guidance, it leads us to our next step in spiritual growth and ultimately helps us become masters of our own lives.

For me, this experience helped explain the reality of the ECK Masters and dreams. I also learned a little bit about the bigger plan in the evolution of Soul—and my part in it. My sense of abandonment disappeared, and I gained a greater level of confidence and certainty in my everyday life. My heart and mind resonated with this newly found wisdom. I found it remarkable that the ECK Masters care enough to assist us in the smallest aspects of our lives and in the most seemingly insignificant details of our growth and advancement.

It is still a most profound truth that fills me with awe and gratitude.

14

What Is It That You Wish?

Inner Guidance for the Greatest Vision of Ourselves

If you want something from life, first of all you have to earn it. But you also have to be open to the gifts life is willing to give you, and that means you have to ask for them.

—Harold Klemp
The Golden Heart[20]

---

*I*nner meetings with the Mahanta and other ECK Masters became more and more frequent. And the more I practiced my intent to meet nightly with the ECK Masters, the more vivid my dreams became.

One particular night, I was questioning my goals as Soul. What was I really here for? What was my highest and most divine purpose in this life?

As I fell asleep, I soared immediately into a very clear dream. In the dream, two beings approached me from a distance. They were deeply engaged in conversation. As they drew near, I recognized them as ECK Masters. One was the modern-day founder of Eckankar,

Paul Twitchell, and the other was a Tibetan ECK Master named Rebazar Tarzs.

The dream was replete with fine detail. Paul Twitchell wore a light-blue shirt with the sleeves rolled up slightly. He had piercing blue eyes, he looked fresh and young, and I could hear the lilt of a Southern accent in his voice. The scenery was picturesque beyond words. There were mountain peaks so high I could barely distinguish their tops. A pristine blue sky was daubed with a few swirling white clouds. In a meadow of brilliant emerald green, dotted with pink and purple flowering trees, I stood in anticipation and waited for these teachers to approach and greet me.

But as they stepped in front of me, they continued with their conversation, not even glancing up. They were about to pass me, when someone else walked up beside me. It was a dear friend from my waking life.

The ECK Masters stopped talking. They looked right at me and both nodded a greeting. Rebazar Tarzs smiled gently and asked, "What is it that you wish?"

I didn't answer. I was too aware of my friend's presence. Perhaps he had a much greater need than I did. Turning to him, I encouraged him to speak up. I hoped he would ask for the healing that I felt he urgently needed.

But he was silent.

Rebazar was studying me. He said clearly, once again, "You called for us. What is it that you wish?"

Hearing this Master's request for the second time, I made one last effort. I looked quickly at my friend, still trying to encourage him to speak. He firmly folded his arms over his chest as he looked at Rebazar and me. "I ask for nothing," he said.

Rebazar then nodded at my friend and said quietly, "And so it shall be."

My dear friend, for his own reasons, was standing before two ECK Masters and declining to ask for help. I looked at him with compassion. His face appeared distant and alone. This was not his time. He would not ask.

I suddenly understood what is meant by the concept that we must ask in order to receive. Such is the love and detachment of these beings that they will never invade our personal or spiritual space. They will come to our aid only if it is truly our own personal desire and request.

Still wanting desperately to help my friend, I longed to intervene. However, my inner guidance was warning me that I should not ask for anything for another person. Like the ECK Masters, we also must learn to respect the spiritual freedom of others. I was being given a lesson in detachment or noninterference: an individual who wants help must personally request it and be open to it.

*T*his dream had begun with a spiritual exercise. Days earlier, I had read about a technique of placing pictures of ECK Masters near one's bed and focusing on them before falling asleep. I decided to give this a try. Just recently, I had been given a gift—colorful drawings of four ECK Masters. After framing the pictures, I put them on the wall right by my bed.

So for this spiritual exercise, I focused on the pictures of these four ECK Masters: Paul Twitchell, with his blue eyes; Gopal Das, with long blond hair; Rebazar Tarzs, with swarthy skin and a maroon robe; and Lai Tsi, an Asian gentleman with a long white beard.

Contemplating their faces sweetly just before I fell asleep, I whispered a request for their help, guidance, and assistance. I also sang HU softly to myself as I dozed off, remembering that this word, HU, is a name for God that can be used to help spiritualize the consciousness. In this state, I drifted off to sleep.

I did this exercise night after night, and on the third night I had the dream. It was so real, it was as if I were wide awake. It was as compelling and concrete as any scene in everyday life—yet even more spectacular.

My friend disappeared as quickly as he'd arrived. I stood alone with the two Masters, looking at the faces of both Rebazar and Paul. They appeared powerful yet eternally patient. "What is it that you wish?" Rebazar urged again.

It felt like the rest of my lifetime on this earth was suddenly at stake. In this ECK Master's question, I sensed a grave impression of urgency, magnitude, and consequence. Goodness! This meeting was no simple occurrence. I suddenly understood inwardly that this was a crossroads, a turning point that would determine the tide of everything to come.

Although I was not sick, requesting a healing seemed to be the only thing I could think of. With a weak smile, I mumbled, "I want a healing, please."

There was a moment of silence. Then Rebazar encouraged me to continue. "Go on," he instructed kindly.

Having just given birth, I did need help in regaining my strength and getting healthy again. Reflecting on that, a healing now sounded like a reasonable idea that could have long-range benefit. Encouraged to say more, I tried to be a bit more specific. "I want a healing of my physical body, my strength and energy."

Rebazar smiled. "Go on."

I was supposed to ask for more? There was no time

for reflection. I felt like I was being asked to redesign my life right there and then! The two ECK Masters were standing quietly, looking at me, waiting.

I boldly replied, "I would like a healing of my body, my health, my career, my home, my finances . . . and my closet." I added the last item feebly, with a bit of a giggle. New clothes might seem like a trivial concern, but to me they were important after having just delivered a baby. I waited to see if I had offended Rebazar or Paul by adding so many specifics, including my desire for a new wardrobe.

Rebazar looked at me with gentle amusement, nodded again, and repeated, "Go on."

Panic began to set in. I had no idea what I was supposed to say now. I took a brief moment to reflect and then realized that certainly the biggest issue in my life was one I was hesitant to even examine: my shaky marriage. I wanted more than anything to give my child a wonderful family.

"I would like a healing of my heart, my home, and my family."

Again Rebazar nodded, smiled sweetly, and said, "Go on."

What? Hadn't I thought of everything? Surely I had asked for what I wanted and needed. I wondered if I had missed something that Rebazar could see in my heart. Maybe all of this was too trivial. I would have to be even more creative. It was like a quiz where all the possibilities of the universe were open to me but only the exact right answers would do.

Realizing I needed to take a step up, I opened myself to greater inner guidance right there in the dream. Suddenly, it came to me. Out of the blue, I understood that I really did have all the possibilities of the universe open to me. I just had to raise my consciousness to the level of acceptance to which I was being guided. Now I knew what to ask.

"I want a healing of my entire life—past, present, and future—on every level, including the physical, emotional, mental, karmic, and spiritual," I said.

Rebazar nodded enthusiastically, as if I had finally caught on.

Yet there was more. I detected the slightest trace of amusement as he nodded and said once more, "Go on."

I laughed. Apparently, they were going to work with me until I truly learned this lesson. Such patience! I hoped to be up to the task.

Even as I stood there in the dream, I suddenly felt a surge of energy flowing through me, a feeling I recognized from my spiritual exercises as an increased flow of Divine Spirit, or the ECK. Again, I was filled with the certainty that this was a significant meeting that would help me in every possible way and in every area of my life.

Gratitude flooded my heart. "I ask for love," I said quietly, "and peace, happiness, freedom, wisdom, and health. I ask to serve in the greatest way possible, and I ask for all things that are for my greatest good and the greatest good of all. I ask for the fulfillment of my highest possible destiny in this lifetime and for all the guidance, protection, and direction I will need to guarantee that fulfillment. I ask for all this."

Not a beat passed between my latest enormous request and his response: "Go on."

Was there anything left to say? Hadn't I proven my willingness to open my heart to the guidance and blessings of God? Apparently I needed a little more help with my inner guidance in this extraordinary experience! With these great ECK Masters gazing intently at me, I had to stop and contemplate what to do or say next.

As I did so, diving deeper within myself for the answer, I realized a profound truth. This awareness finally began to seep into my entire being. The answer was this: I couldn't possibly know everything I might truly need or want, but the ECK Masters knew.

Harold Klemp teaches that these spiritual travelers are able to see a higher picture of our greatest potential as Soul, in this lifetime or any other. They can guide us to our highest destiny, if we are open.

Rebazar knew my heart. He knew me better than I knew myself! He knew exactly what it was that I couldn't fully comprehend—and he was here to help me achieve it, if I would ask.

"If there is anything which I have forgotten that is for my greatest good, anything of which you are aware that I am not, I ask for that too. I ask for your help. Please." I added, "Take and make the most of me. I ask you to work with me at any time—past, present, and future—in whatever way is best, whether I am aware of what I need or not. I surrender to your guidance."

Feelings of peace and exhilaration enveloped me like a cloak as I uttered my final words.

It was a moment of true humility and surrender, signifying my willingness to yield to Divine Spirit's greater awareness and wisdom, to stop denying myself and assessing life from a limited viewpoint. It was a lesson I needed to learn from several different angles, yet this was an open door, and I was going through.

At last, a look passed between Rebazar and Paul. They both nodded and smiled at each other. Their work with me was complete. Then, bending at the waist, Rebazar bowed in my direction responding with great dignity, "And so it shall be."

Paul nodded at me, smiling with a twinkle in those sapphire eyes of his. I stood quietly and watched them walk away into a swirling mist.

To surrender to my own greatest good and experience unconditional love in return from these two ECK Masters was a definitive experience in inner guidance for me. I knew I would receive all the blessings I had requested, and all life would change for the better.

15

Taking the Next Step in Spiritual Unfoldment:
Inner Guidance and Karmic Release

The path of ECK is an adventurous one. Everything that is given to you is given because you are able to handle it. No matter what comes up in your life, you have enough inner strength or the Master wouldn't have given you that next step in your spiritual unfoldment.

—Harold Klemp
How to Find God[21]

---

*W*e are each a unique spark of God, as Soul. The ECK Masters know this, and they gently guide us toward ever higher realizations of ourselves as spiritual beings. Sometimes, to get to the next step in spiritual unfoldment, we have to go through challenging doorways. We have to let go of something that's holding us back.

After nine years of teaching, my inner guidance had been nudging me toward change. This was a surprise. I loved teaching, but the inner guidance was persistent.

I decided to leave my current position at the end of the year and take a much-needed break.

My marriage to Jon had since dissolved, and I would be spending the summer vacation on Hilton Head Island at my mother's home. My daughter, Sarah, and I would enjoy a long holiday on the beach.

Vacation was bliss. Weeks slipped by. I had intended to spend some time during my break looking for a new teaching position, but July passed and much of August too, and I realized there might not be a position available this late in the summer. For many schools, classes had already started. I had enjoyed the holiday so much that I had not even noticed the passage of time and my dwindling resources.

One day in late August, I sat down to ask for inner guidance on the next step. I closed my eyes, took a few deep breaths, and relaxed into a spiritual exercise. As the sound of HU resonated through me, I let go of my fear and worry. I imagined myself conversing with the Inner Master, and I posed several questions inwardly.

If I were going to continue my teaching career, where would I find work at this late date? Should I stay on this little idyllic island and try to fit into a small school here? Or should I try to find another job entirely?

"HU-U-U-U," I sang quietly on each outgoing breath.

Only a few minutes into this process, the doorbell rang. I considered ignoring it to continue my spiritual exercise, but the bell at the front door rang urgently, again and again. This was odd; no one used that entrance to my mother's home.

I went to answer the door. A uniformed man stood there, smiling broadly.

He asked my name and then said he was really glad to find me. With a sigh of relief, he laughingly mentioned that I was a difficult person to track down. He had a telegram for me! I'd never received a telegram in my life.

It was from a professor in the Department of Education at Indiana University. Because of my interests and specific academic qualifications, he was recommending me for an administrative and teaching position at a high school near Cincinnati, Ohio. The director of that school program had resigned, for personal reasons, just a few days after classes had started, and they needed a replacement.

Responding immediately to this opportunity, I called to accept the offer. The principal agreed to employ me at the high end of the salary range, plus pay me a bonus for agreeing to take over the program at the last minute. I would have to pack without delay. Marveling at my good fortune, and at how quickly my inner questions had been answered, I thanked the Mahanta for everything.

What a miraculous event! I took a moment to sit down and sing HU. Joyfully, I expressed my gratitude. My quandary was solved, my future was secure, and I was off on a new and exciting adventure.

Mom waved good-bye as Sarah and I boarded a plane the next morning. In fewer than twenty-four hours, our lives had been perfectly rearranged. The new position was at a large and innovative public school. It was my tenth year of teaching, and I would be in charge of the new program and would also teach—a perfect career combination for me.

But soon I would learn that something was changing. A karmic release was happening, and it would be my last year in teaching. It was just as my inner guidance had said, ten years before.

On my first day at the new school, an imposing and eye-catching sign featuring the name of the program was just being hung above the school door. As this sign was slowly hoisted into position by a small crane, it temporarily swung upside down. I looked at it curiously, leaning my head to one side, trying to read it. No one had actually mentioned the name of the program I was now administering, so I wanted to see what the sign said. There were only four letters: N-O-V-A.

That was the name of this new alternative high-school program. NOVA, a luminous star! I liked that image, and I called out to the crane operator, "That's a great name!"

Then the sign dropped slightly and was hoisted again. It swayed this way and that while I stared at it, mesmerized. Suddenly, my heart sank. Looking at the sign upside down and backward, as the crane operator tried to rebalance it, I read the name quite differently now: Avon.

Avon is Nova spelled backward, an anadrome. How remarkable! Avon was the name of the school where I held my very *first* teaching position. Suddenly it seemed as if my life had come full circle. Here I was at the beginning of my tenth year of teaching, remembering the inner guidance I had received years before: "You will teach for ten years, and then you will teach no longer."

With a sinking heart, I reflected on the significance of what was occurring here. Avon High School was where I had started my career, and the Nova program might somehow mark the end—my *last* school, if this insight into my future were to come to pass.

Despite my conflict and confusion, deep inside I felt the reassurance of inner guidance. I felt the prophecy would come true in my life and somehow work out for the best—just as so many other inner messages had in the past.

*C*hecking the validity of our inner guidance both inwardly and outwardly is essential. I decided I would just lightly hold on to the message and see what might come of it. If this were to be my last year of teaching, I knew something even better would be waiting for me.

Perhaps some sort of a karmic release would happen. As I looked at my inner guidance on this potentially impending change in my life, I sensed that behind it were forces set in motion long ago, all designed to lead me to my highest potential as Soul. Although I did not know what these ancient forces were, I prepared myself inwardly for whatever might come my way.

I would simply expect the best and put my attention on the present, trusting in the benevolent hand of God in my life. That is the way it is when we allow ourselves to be watched over and guided in the direction of our greatest good. The outcome, when it turned up, would certainly be most amazing.

I loved the school, contributed much to the program, and took the next step in my career as an educator. Yet this was also the year of my near-death accident: Sarah and I would be hit by a drunk driver. Sarah would remain unharmed, while I would be seriously injured. It was also at the end of this tenth year of teaching, while recuperating from the accident, that I would hear about a new opportunity.

16

Letting Go of Anger, Accepting Grace:

Inner Guidance through a Waking Dream

The daily struggles that life presents are opportunities to cultivate spiritual grace.

—Harold Klemp
Wisdom of the Heart, Book 1[22]

---

arah and I were really enjoying Cincinnati. We had moved into an apartment in a very beautiful part of the city. Living near historic Mount Adams allowed us to enjoy nature and play together at the spacious, well-manicured park. There was a wonderful fine-arts museum just a short walk from my front door. I immediately felt at home in this bustling area. A brilliant autumn was already at its peak when we arrived in late September.

I liked this area of the country, and I enjoyed where I lived and where I worked. However, the distance from our uptown home to the suburban high school where I was employed was another matter altogether! It was quite a long drive, and to arrive on time for my first class

149

each morning, I had to leave very early and fight the traffic. Still, it was a price I was willing to pay to live near the heart of the city.

As a single mother, I found it a major undertaking to get my sleepy daughter up, dressed, fed, and ready to go out the door with her lunch, toys, and other paraphernalia. Then, after loading all my school papers and books into the car, to drive us safely in the early morning darkness to our destinations. Five days a week, I would drop Sarah off at preschool and then try to get to work early enough to prepare for a busy day of teaching. By the time I arrived in my classroom, just before 7:15, I was already stressed by the hassles of the commute.

Daily pressures were permeating my heart and mind. I felt I was doing the best I could outwardly with the demands of life, but I clearly needed a new spiritual perspective.

As a student of Eckankar, I enjoyed my daily spiritual exercises, especially singing HU. HU allowed me to stay in a calm and untroubled state of mind, most of the time. The spiritual exercises also helped me create a greater inner awareness and mastery over my life.

One particular morning, I decided to ask a specific question during my spiritual exercise. "How can I live in a greater state of peace, harmony, and happiness," I asked the Inner Master, "while being less affected by the stress and strain of everyday events?"

After posing this question, I continued to contemplate, and I sang HU several times. While I softly chanted this ancient name for God, I felt a strong stirring of love. I almost immediately moved into a deep and expansive awareness. A simple question floated through my mind and heart:

If there were one simple thing that I could keep in mind that would help me throughout this entire lifetime, what would it be?

The answer, the briefest inner guidance, came immediately. It came as one word: *grace*. I wondered about that word. My mind could not wrap itself around *grace* as my answer. The word *grace* just didn't have any special meaning for me, and it was not anything I expected. I thought I might be given a word that had more immediate spiritual meaning for me—like *love* or *harmony* or *perseverance*.

What might the word *grace* actually mean in my busy, modern life?

The word stuck in my thoughts as I prepared to make my daily dash out of the house with Sarah. What did this word have to do with me—a hardworking, single mom who was struggling to make her way in a demanding world?

I decided to contemplate on this later. Right now I needed to gather up Sarah and our things and head out into the day. I made a mental note to look up the word *grace* in the dictionary as soon as I possibly could.

I snapped the seat belt around Sarah and dragged myself into the car. As I pulled out into traffic, I listened to my daughter singing a little song in the backseat, and I relaxed a bit just hearing the sweetness in her voice.

I was about to experience a unique form of spiritual guidance called a waking dream. Harold Klemp writes, "Sometimes the Holy Spirit will arrange for an outer confirmation of what was revealed in your inner worlds, in your heart. This connection between the inner and the outer is what we call the waking dream."[23]

Making my way easily through the downtown area, I headed north. When I entered the on-ramp, I could see that the major highway was already busy with traffic. I gathered speed to merge smoothly and signaled my move into the open lane.

Glancing into the rearview mirror, I was shocked to see a huge white truck coming up rapidly behind me. It appeared the driver did not see my car about to enter the lane. He wasn't moving over or slowing down at all. I was moving too fast to try to stop, but if I proceeded to merge, the truck would surely collide with my car.

There was nowhere else for me to go! Instinctively, I swerved off the road and over the narrow shoulder of the highway. I was forced to drive onto a grassy slope just above an imposing ditch.

As I made these frightening maneuvers, Sarah continued to sing in the backseat. Her little song was in stark contrast to the drama unfolding on the highway.

Somehow, I managed to bring the car safely to a stop, but we were now sitting at a steep and precarious angle. My heart was racing as I assessed the situation, but I forced myself to collect my thoughts. I calculated that if I could get the car moving fast enough along the embankment, I could get back over the shoulder and onto the highway, hopefully without needing emergency assistance.

I first looked around to judge whether I could make the maneuver safely, then took my shot at reentering the highway.

Cautiously, I accelerated and was greatly relieved to find myself moving quite smoothly along the grass. I steered my car onto the shoulder and proceeded to merge into the flow of traffic. Shaken but determined, I gained speed and moved steadily along the highway.

Now I had the situation under control, yet I lapsed into a state of anger. I imagined the very worst about the truck driver and his intentions. How dare that truck force us off the road! We could have been killed! The driver didn't even stop to see if we were OK. How could he be so callous, so reckless? I really wanted to give him a piece of my mind.

Then something happened, a flash of remembered guidance. I recalled the word *grace*.

I recalled the peaceful stillness I had experienced while singing HU earlier in the morning. I breathed deeply, and as I motored along, I sang HU quietly a few times. The inner calm began to return.

As this feeling of peace returned, I remembered an important fact of life: in some way, everything that happens is for our own spiritual benefit and growth. My daughter and I were safe and sound, not harmed in a single way. Indeed, we'd clearly been protected from a terrible collision. Gratitude began to seep in and illuminate all the dark corners of my mind and emotions.

And as I drove along, I again pondered how the word *grace* had just popped into my inner awareness that very morning. If I were responding to this incident with grace, I would definitely be thinking about how grateful I was that we were unharmed. I might even stop to consider that the truck driver perhaps never even saw my car. He probably didn't know that he had nearly run a woman and her child into a ditch. After all, the highway was packed with rush-hour traffic, all vying for the same limited space. His attention was likely elsewhere on the road as he tried to drive safely.

Further, I realized that the truck driver was also Soul, and, like me, he was probably doing his very best in the moment. Taking a few deep breaths, I was able to slip into a calm and comforted state. At last, I felt nothing but a profound sense of gratitude flooding through me.

My car was now effortlessly heading up a long rise. The white truck was likely not that far ahead of me. This incline always slowed down the larger vehicles; I'd probably overtake the truck on the long stretch uphill.

It would be easy to recognize the large semi that had forced me off the road; the truck and trailer were both bright white. I imagined what I would do when I passed him. With my new attitude, I wouldn't glare at the driver and show anger. Whether he knew what had happened or not didn't matter to me now. I would smile and nod my head, acknowledging him. We had shared a threatening moment and had all come out of it unscathed, even if he didn't realize it.

This was my plan: I would see his truck and look over at him and simply feel love for all life. I would keep a positive attitude, full of gratitude because all of us were safe and sound.

I saw the long white truck as I approached it. With a smile on my face, I took a deep breath and began to pass. As I glanced over to try to see the driver's face, I could hardly believe my eyes. I couldn't see the driver yet, but what I did see was a pristine white truck with one word painted on its side, in giant black letters: GRACE! It was a Grace truck, from a manufacturing company with a private trucking line.

When I saw the driver, I was grinning like the Cheshire cat! I was beaming, laughing, and shaking my head. The driver couldn't help noticing me. He smiled back and nodded in my direction, giving me a little wave.

Of course, he had no idea what had happened. And he would never know how instrumental he'd been in the delivery of a crystal-clear spiritual message—a waking-dream message that it had taken an entire eighteen-wheeler to deliver!

$\mathcal{W}$aking dreams are a wonderful way Divine Spirit nudges us to let go of old habits that are limiting our perspective. For me, letting go of anger and accepting grace that day changed everything. I knew from the teachings of Eckankar that my attitude affected every aspect of my existence. When I am in a state of peace and joy, I easily attract experiences of peace and joy. When tense and full of worry, doubt, or fear, I certainly cut myself off from the guidance and love that are always available.

To receive God's love and the divine flow of the universe, we have to align ourselves with it.

The Mahanta, the Inner Master, works with us to help disarm any potentially damaging karmic situations. Yet, we are ultimately responsible for obeying spiritual law and working consciously to help create our highest good. This was a liberating revelation.

With this knowledge I could begin to take greater responsibility for creating the life I really desired. I wanted a life that was more in harmony with the spiritual states of grace, love, joy, wisdom, and freedom.

The Grace truck was all about relaxing the tensions of my life. Things became easier and more pleasant for me as I learned to relax more. I trusted that I was receiving help inwardly from the Mahanta, my inner guide, as I consciously sought to also be more responsible for my own life. My appreciation for life's simple gifts grew, and my heart seemed to gain a greater capacity to express love and gratitude.

I was amazed at how a seemingly subtle shift in attitude could produce such notable results.

$\mathcal{I}$n the months that followed the Grace truck incident, I gained deeper insights into the spiritual principle behind that experience. In studying the teachings of Eckankar, I have learned that Soul exists because of God's love for It. Grace is divine love and protection that is freely available for all people. To receive the grace of God is to be blessed. The fact is, we are all blessed. We are watched over, guided, and protected at all times, whether we are aware of it or not.

"The waking dream is usually an outer experience given by the Mahanta. Its purpose is to point to a spiritual lesson through an example in your outer life,"[24] writes Harold Klemp. I'll always remember that morning I met the Grace truck and its driver, the morning I learned an important lesson about the mystery of life and the blessings that surround us.

I had another moment of surprise when I researched the word *grace* in the library. It turns out that my name, Anne, means "grace."

I laughed at the subtle play of Spirit at work. This knowledge brought more breadth to my experience and personalized it even more.

17

Miracles I Can
Do in a Minute:

Inner Guidance and the
Application of Spiritual Principles

*Often people are afraid to follow their inner
guidance. It sounds like such a foolish thing to
do, especially if they have to face other people and
explain why they are doing what they are doing.*

—Harold Klemp
The Slow Burning Love of God[25]

"You can't just *create* miracles, or they wouldn't
call them miracles! And no one can do the
impossible," my students were insisting.

They needed something to shake them up.
Friday afternoon, following an inner message, I'd written these challenging words on the blackboard in bold letters: "Miracles I can do in a minute. The impossible takes about three days."

The words were not mine, and I was not really sure who said or wrote them, but the principle was intriguing. I had asked what might work with this group to help

157

open their eyes a bit, and this little bit of philosophy is what I was guided to inwardly.

My students argued, but I knew they wanted to believe that this spiritual principle was true. Right now, however, they were challenging me.

The discussion centered on the proposition that we have far more control over our own lives than we believe, if we follow spiritual principles. By stepping into agreement with the Divine, we move into a world of opportunities greater than any we might otherwise have expected or experienced in our lives. This concept pushed the students right to the limit of belief.

They challenged me for an example from my own life. I started to tell them some of the stories from my past. "No, not stories! We want you to prove it now," they insisted. They wanted more; they wanted to witness this principle in action.

Collectively they demanded, "Just do it for yourself! Find a goal you want, and show us how it works."

Suddenly I was in the hot seat. I needed to somehow demonstrate the truth of what I was saying. I felt the pressure.

I knew that one of the most important things we can do is learn to apply spiritual principles in our lives at all times. In fact, there is nothing worse, when attempting to accept responsibility for our own lives, than thinking that miracles are something that only happened in biblical times. This was something I wanted to teach these students—to really demonstrate—and they were insistent that I put it into practice *now*.

Was there some goal, some little seemingly impossible thing, I might achieve as they watched me apply this spiritual principle?

Just then, my inner guidance offered me a direction. Inwardly, I was being shown something I had been

Miracles I Can Do in a Minute:
Inner Guidance and the   159
Application of Spiritual Principles

longing for recently. I had wished I could go sailing in a hot-air balloon and enjoy the splendor of the autumn colors from on high. But I had dismissed this goal as frivolous and too expensive for me right now.

Smiling at the students, I said, "I want a hot-air balloon ride. I don't have money for this adventure. Yet, here is how I understand I can help manifest that ride: Imagine a goal clearly; assume you already have it— really feel it and accept it and imbue the image with love; and then surrender the outcome for the good of all. And it will manifest if it is for the greatest good."

The students still appeared mildly skeptical, but I continued, "If we want our goal to manifest in whatever way is really best, we must surrender it to Divine Spirit. For the surrender part, what I like to declare is, 'If not this, then something greater!' We might also surrender it to the will of God by saying, 'Thy will be done.'"

Pausing to answer questions as I went, I added, "If we imagine the best outcome, and then surrender it for the good of all, we open the door to miracles. Of course, we must follow our inner guidance and act accordingly. We have to do our part and then allow the new desire to come into reality. Just do all we can do, and then see what happens."

They wanted application of the law, not just theory. That was fair. "OK, here we go," I said. "I assume I have my hot-air balloon ride. I am in the balloon, floating along, happy and free."

I described myself sailing over the Ohio River, brushing the tops of the trees in a vividly colored hot-air balloon. I said, "It's big and bright and beautiful, and I am in the balloon, smiling and jubilant! I feel the sense of freedom, soaring through the air. I love every minute of it. Look at the birds below! Look at the treetops. How wonderful is this?"

The students were mesmerized by my images. "Ah, this is fabulous," I declared, as if I were already sailing through the air. "I am experiencing my hot-air balloon ride, and I am grateful! And now I surrender the whole picture with love, and I expect either this or something greater." Smiles filled the room as many of the students caught the idea and felt the reality of the scene I had described.

This was Friday. If the impossible takes about three days, we had until my first class on Monday morning.

"I'll research balloon rides and keep my attention positively focused on this picture," I said. "I'll stay open and follow my inner guidance. But to manifest a first-class hot-air balloon ride will definitely be a miracle for me now."

I ended the discussion by explaining, "The final step is surrender. We can simply say, 'May the blessings be.'"

The school bell rang, and we closed the class, keyed up with curiosity about our grand experiment and the potential results.

$\mathcal{T}$eaching in this new position in Cincinnati was very stimulating. As I'd done in other schools, I used philosophy to inspire the students and shared it generously on the classroom walls. Uplifting quotes filled the room—quotes by Socrates, Plato, Emerson, Thoreau, and now also Paul Twitchell, Eckankar's founder.

Twitchell's writings especially seemed to move the students, giving a foundation to comprehend life from a greater perspective. He presented an enhanced understanding of our spiritual nature and provided tools to lead an individual to a greater mastery of life.

The students were always curious and questioning, thirsting for more. Responding to their growing interest,

Miracles I Can Do in a Minute:
Inner Guidance and the   161
Application of Spiritual Principles

I had posted the two enticing lines: "Miracles I can do in a minute. The impossible takes about three days."

Now my students had confronted me with this whole hot-air balloon challenge, and according to the three-day formula for the impossible, I had until Monday morning to get my ride figured out!

When I left the school building that afternoon, I could not help but wonder about the wisdom of what I had set in motion. I was more than a little curious to see what the outcome would be!

After a quick supper with my daughter, I went to the coin-operated laundry nearby. There, a young man approached me, selling raffle tickets for a children's charity. He had only one more ticket to sell, he mentioned hopefully.

I started to shake my head no, since I did not have very much money left. But suddenly my inner guidance unmistakably advised me: "Buy that ticket." Was I supposed to support this cause? It sounded worthy, but after my recent move, I was very short of money. Yet, my inner guidance was clear: "Take that ticket!"

As I relinquished my last five dollars, I was astonished at myself. This was decades ago, when five dollars was a lot of money for me. I did not want to even think about how tight cash was at this point. For I was now left with absolutely no money to spare until my next payday and would have to make do with whatever I had.

I took the ticket, wrote my name and phone number on it, and kept the stub. For a fleeting moment, I wondered about my judgment. Yet, foolish though it appeared, I actually felt really good about buying the ticket. I had followed my guidance, and I felt pleased with my actions. I would make it till my next paycheck, and I was helping children in need.

The next morning, Saturday, I woke up intending

to inquire about hot-air balloon rides. But before I had even eaten breakfast, the phone rang.

"You won the charity grand prize!" said the caller. "You've won a spectacular hot-air balloon ride over the Ohio River and the city of Cincinnati. It's tomorrow in the late afternoon, just before sunset. Congratulations!"

*O*verjoyed, I saw that in my attempt to demonstrate this spiritual principle to my students, something amazing had happened. Divine Spirit was illustrating the spiritual laws in a more outstanding manner than I might ever have imagined. And it had not even taken three days!

What had happened here? The inner nudge, my guidance, had pushed me forward. Because the raffle ticket was for needy children, my heart had opened. Love had poured in, and I was willing to offer up my last five dollars unconditionally and without any expectation of winning anything.

Yet, miracle of miracles, just hours later the balloon ride was a reality.

*W*hen I arrived at the balloon site on Sunday afternoon, a large crowd had already gathered. Making my way through the milling throng, I proceeded toward the brightly colored balloon, which was primed and ready to go.

To my surprise, a plethora of dignitaries waited in anticipation of meeting me! I was very warmly welcomed and immediately introduced to the media. The television reporters wanted before-and-after interviews with me! There were politicians, celebrities—and *me*.

And a short time later, there I was, sailing over the

Miracles I Can Do in a Minute:
Inner Guidance and the   163
Application of Spiritual Principles

Ohio River and the trees dressed in their autumn finery. It truly took my breath away. This miracle was far beyond my creation; it was a miracle of inner guidance.

In the midst of all this, I clearly recognized the handiwork of the Inner Master, the Mahanta, opening a spiritual door for my students. I smiled quietly in gratitude for the inner guidance that opened my heart to more love and so wisely urged me to spend my last five dollars on a cause that was far more worthy than I knew.

Many of the students saw the outcome of our Friday classroom discussion on Sunday night's ten o'clock news. Then, on Monday morning, it was also in the newspaper.

The students were completely awestruck with the spiritual mechanism by which this little miracle had come about. "How did that all happen?" they asked. And when we talked about it this time, they definitely paid attention.

Even more faithful now to my inner guidance, I continued to witness the many practical benefits of applying the spiritual principles, the laws of life that are taught in Eckankar.

18

Men in the House:

Asking for Inner Guidance Opens a Door to Spiritual Worlds

Spirit is always with us, always guiding, always protecting, always attempting to bring joy and make our life better, but that doesn't mean that we are always aware and listening.

—Harold Klemp
How to Find God[26]

"*M*ommy, there are men in the house!"

When my daughter, Sarah, woke me that night, I was sound asleep. She had crawled into my bed and was sitting up next to me.

"Wake up, Mommy, wake up!" she said as she tugged on my arm. It was midnight. I was barely able to rouse myself. I looked at Sarah to see if she were sick or just wanting to sleep with me. Then, I heard the words she was repeating, and I was alarmed.

"Mommy, there are men in the house!"

Quickly, I sat up in bed and whispered, "Men? Where did you see men, Sarah?"

"They are right here at the foot of your bed, Mommy. See them?"

165

My panic melted away. I saw only the sheer curtains that covered the bedroom windows. The blinds were open; the room was illumined by a nearby streetlight. There were definitely no men standing at the foot of my bed. I assumed that my daughter had been dreaming. "No, I don't see anyone, Honey. Are you sure you see them?"

"Yes, Mommy, there are three of them. They are Masters."

While I was shocked to hear her tell me that she saw Masters, I was eager to hear about whatever she thought she was seeing.

"Why would you say they are Masters, Sarah?"

"Because, Mommy, they are all in light."

This amazed me. I wanted to understand more. "Tell me what you see. Describe them to me, Honey."

"Look, Mommy, you can see them! They are so clear. There are three of them, and they are here to see you."

"Here to see me? Sarah, I'm sorry, but I don't see them. Please tell me what they look like."

"One has his picture on the book you're reading," she explained. That would be Paul Twitchell, I thought. I had shown her his picture. To my mind, Sarah's mention of Paul Twitchell invalidated her story. She had been told he was an ECK Master, so naturally she could be imagining him.

"OK, Honey, that's nice," I said. "But let's go back to sleep."

As I made my way more deeply into an understanding of Eckankar, the question of the reality of the ECK Masters continued to arouse wonder in my mind. I had asked for more guidance on this subject. I tried to be open; I tried to listen. Yet, this was the hardest

Men in the House:
Asking for Inner Guidance   167
Opens a Door to Spiritual Worlds

part of Eckankar for me to understand and accept.

Who are they? I questioned. Were they truly real? How do they come to be in their position of Mastership? These were my queries, and I asked inwardly for deeper guidance and insights into this matter.

I was about to discover a new dimension of guidance—about to see that my sincere questions to the Inner Master were opening me to a new level of spiritual awareness.

"*M*ommy, they are here to see you!" Sarah protested. "Please try to see them."

Because of her plaintive sincerity, I decided to pay more attention. "OK, Sarah, tell me about the other two."

"One has dark hair," my daughter chattered happily. "And the other is the most light of all."

"Light? Well, tell me about him, please."

She spoke hurriedly. "He is the most light of all! He is made all out of light, and he has a big stick made of light, and it is so big it goes right through the ceiling and out of the house!"

My pulse quickened. I remembered the date, October 22, 1981. It was the ECK Spiritual New Year, the time when that mystery of all mysteries might occur— the appointment of a new Living ECK Master in the inner and outer worlds of God.

I certainly did not understand how a new Living ECK Master is selected. It also sounded so extraordinary. Yet, much of what I had experienced in Eckankar was far from the ordinary and quite impressive, so I held an open mind.

Could Sarah be describing the spiritual Rod of ECK Power that is held by the Living ECK Master? If she were talking about *that* "stick," then this person might be a new Living ECK Master, and the Rod of ECK Power might have been transferred to him this very night. Could that possibly be? And why might a new Living ECK Master be appearing in our bedroom at midnight?

"Tell me more about him, Sarah," I encouraged her.

"He's wearing a really big coat, and it's made out of light too, and it is so beautiful it makes me want to cry."

"Are they all wearing coats of light?" I asked.

I understood that through the mouth of a babe, I might be learning about one of the most auspicious occasions in all the worlds of God. I had asked for guidance and answers, and the response was more profound than I thought possible.

"No, only he's wearing one. But it is not really a coat; it's made out of light and has big swirls of light in it, and I like looking at it. It's so pretty."

Was she seeing the Living ECK Master with the mantle that is worn only by the Mahanta? I was astounded even at the possibility. "Tell me more about him, Sarah."

"He has brown hair and looks young and modern, Mommy."

"Modern?" I asked. "What do you mean by modern?"

"He's wearing glasses."

"Glasses!" My hopes were dashed. In my mind, the glasses proved that this was some sort of dream. I tried to gently explain to Sarah: "If he were an ECK Master, Sweetie, he would *not* wear glasses. He would get his eyes fixed or something!"

Sarah never took her attention off the foot of the bed. She jabbed me in the ribs with her elbow and loudly whispered, "Mommy, they can hear you!"

I laughed. She did not want me to offend them.

Men in the House:
Asking for Inner Guidance   169
Opens a Door to Spiritual Worlds

Sarah once again garnered my total attention, and I decided it wouldn't hurt to listen. "OK, sorry. Tell me all about the young and modern one."

"He is here to see you. He is trying to talk to you, Mommy."

Trying to talk to me? I had asked for guidance! Was this an ECK Master, in an ethereal or supraphysical body, truly trying to speak to me? Were Masters here to guide me to a new level of awareness and understanding?

I tried to fine-tune my inner and outer vision to see if I could become more aware of anything or anyone in the room. I felt as if I were squinting inwardly for a sign of anything—a flicker, or even a glimpse of what my daughter was seeing.

"Oh, I'm so sorry, Honey, but please let him know that I can't see or hear him. I am trying," I admitted. I strained to see but was unable to catch even the faintest flicker of anything.

"He has brown hair," Sarah went on. I slumped down in my bed, wearily. "I'm sorry I can't see or hear anything, Sarah, but you sit and talk with them while I go back to sleep, and you can tell me about it in the morning."

"Mom-m-m-my," Sarah whined, begging me to pay attention and to try harder.

"Sorry, Honey, I can't do it," I mumbled, as I crumpled back into my bedding.

In the spiritual works of Eckankar, it's written there is an unbroken line of spiritual Masters called the Ancient Order of the Vairagi. The word *vairag* implies nonattachment to all things, allowing all Souls unfettered freedom of thought, word, and action. It also signifies an attitude of service to all life. It is said that the head of this ancient order is chosen by God. He is the Living ECK Master and may also be the Mahanta, the greatest spiritual guide, able to work with people inwardly—in dreams, by Soul Travel, or by direct inner contact. I had been made aware of some aspects of this presence and guidance in my life already.

I had read that in Eckankar we don't have to take things on faith; we may start there, but soon faith can be replaced by personal experience and awareness. So, in those early days of membership in Eckankar, I had made another request inwardly: If the Mahanta and the Vairagi ECK Masters are helping me and working with me inwardly, I would personally like to know more about them.

My telephone rang just before dawn. Sarah had awakened me at midnight, so I was still half asleep when I groggily reached for the phone. Who would be calling at this hour?

"Anne, wake up. There's a new Living ECK Master!" It was my friend Maxine, calling from the World Wide of ECK Seminar that was happening on the West Coast that very weekend.

"What!" I yelled. "Does he look kind of young and have brown hair? And does he look *modern* and wear glasses?!"

"Why, yes, that's a reasonable description. Do you know him?" she asked.

Moaning loudly, I explained, "I don't know him personally, but I believe he was here last night and I totally ignored him."

"You saw him?"

"No," I continued, "Sarah saw him plainly, along

Men in the House:
Asking for Inner Guidance   **171**
Opens a Door to Spiritual Worlds

with two other ECK Masters, in our bedroom last night. She said they were here to meet me, but I couldn't see them or hear anything. The new Living ECK Master was here, and I ignored him!"

"Goodness, Anne, how do you know who it was?"

Explaining what happened, I told her what Sarah had described: the big stick made out of light and the coat. My friend was in awe, as I now was.

I had read that ECK Masters can be in many places at once, that they can Soul Travel in a Light body, fully present and aware. It amazed me to think that they had visited my humble abode on the auspicious spiritual occasion of the ECK Spiritual New Year.

They were there to see me. Was it because I had asked? Because I wanted greater guidance to understand their reality? Well, they had my attention now!

If a child saw them, they knew I would accept their reality. It was both my daughter's experience and my own, despite my inability to see and hear what Sarah experienced. I now knew these Masters were authentic. They had been here, and their visit probably meant more to my life than I could yet understand. But of this I was confident: the ECK Masters are real; the Mahanta is real. Yesterday's doubts had vanished and were never to return.

By now, I was beginning to understand and realize that there are eye-opening experiences available to us all—experiences that are so far beyond anything we have previously conceived that they might be shocking to many. The effect this particular experience had on me was one of greater commitment. I was determined to be more vigilant in my spiritual efforts.

Inner guidance, I realized, can be more than warnings, prophecies, and directions for living a more fulfilling life; it can also be spiritual experience that leads to greater awareness of truth.

Delighted, I sensed inwardly that the Mahanta, my inner guide, was nodding in accord with my renewed spiritual understanding and desire.

19

I Knew You Wore Glasses:
Inner Guidance and Further Confirmation

The path of ECK is the path of experience. We start out with faith, we start out with belief, but after a time our faith and belief are replaced by actual experience so that we know.

—Harold Klemp
Journey of Soul[27]

The visit of the new Living ECK Master and other members of the Ancient Order of the Vairagi in their spiritual bodies erased all conscious doubt about the reality of these spiritual teachers. Yet when I heard that there was a major Eckankar seminar scheduled in Chicago the following spring, inwardly I knew I had to attend.

I sensed that at this seminar there would be even more for me to learn—further confirmation of the spiritual truths I was discovering. Following this guidance, I made plans to be there with my daughter.

The new Living ECK Master would be speaking, and I was eager to see this spiritual leader with whom

I had already been having inner experiences. During the drive to the Windy City, Sarah began singing a little song, one she had made up months earlier: "He is the Master. He was he." That's what it sounded like. Other little lines were occasionally added, but it always returned to the same chorus: "He is the Master. He was he." It sounded like a typically nonsensical song made up by a child.

But nothing in our life is there by accident; it is all connected. When we hear the spoken word, and it stands out starkly to us and catches our attention on a spiritual level, it is Golden-tongued Wisdom, a form of inner guidance. This little song, though simple, was definitely catching my attention. Was the Master trying to tell me something? Despite its monotony, I grew to like the little tune even though I didn't understand its meaning.

During the seminar, when it was time for the dinner break on Saturday, I went to the children's room to collect Sarah. As I entered the room, I heard an exclamation from one of the other adults: "Oh look, it's Sarah's mother!"

I found myself surrounded by adults who were all talking at once. One woman asked, "You personally know the new Living ECK Master, don't you?"

Puzzled, I responded, "Actually, no, I don't know him at all."

Another woman offered a detailed account of what was causing the confusion. "Sri Harold, the Living ECK Master, came to visit the children's room. None of us knew he was coming. But all of a sudden, Sarah stood up from the children's circle and ran to the door. Before any of us could catch her, the door opened, Sri Harold stepped through, and she leaped into his arms. She was hugging his neck and shrieking with delight, 'I knew you wore glasses! I knew you did!'

"He looked right at Sarah, called her by name, and gave her a personal message for you—so we figured you *must* know him."

I shook my head and laughed. "No, I don't know him," I explained again. "Please tell me the message that Sri Harold gave Sarah. Did you hear it? Did he say anything else about the glasses?"

"Oh, yes," she assured me. "He said, 'Sarah, please tell your mommy that I am going to try to get my eyes fixed. I am going to the eye doctor very soon and will get contacts or something. OK? Will you tell her for me?' And Sarah agreed, of course, and that was the end of it. They hugged, and he walked around the room, greeting the other children with Sarah at his side, and then he left. We thought you were friends since Sarah knew him."

Humbled, embarrassed, and amused all at once, I understood that Sri Harold had heard me talking to Sarah that night as he stood with us in his inner or Light body. He had heard *exactly* what I'd said to Sarah in our bedroom when she described him, along with the other two ECK Masters, on the evening of October 22, when the Rod of ECK Power was passed.

I had said that if he were a Master, he would get his eyes fixed or something and he wouldn't be wearing glasses. And now he intended to do just that and had responded outwardly. Our new Living ECK Master had quite a keen sense of humor, it seemed. And he was letting me know that that experience was as real as the outer life and that the Inner Master is truly with us.

I had wanted guidance about the Living ECK Master—his lofty spiritual role and how he works—and he wanted to make sure I knew without a doubt that he and the other ECK Masters were real and could be there in my room, while they were simultaneously in the supraphysical world at a ceremony for the new Living ECK Master.

Sri Harold had taken my discourteous and skeptical comments with patience and a light heart. Once again, I was left with the gift of a totally altered consciousness—transformed through the Inner Master's generous response and my young daughter's awareness and recognition of the Mahanta.

I have since learned that these unconditionally loving, freedom-giving, and nonjudgmental ECK Masters often work with us inwardly for years before we know they exist. At some deep level, we may invite and receive their guidance and help in our spiritual journey before we are even aware of it outwardly. No request for spiritual tutelage or inner guidance is ever too insignificant for their attention, as long as our hearts are sincere and open.

$\mathcal{I}$t was on the way home from Chicago that I finally learned the meaning of Sarah's song. At the seminar, I had discovered that the spiritual name of Sri Harold Klemp is Wah Z. Now I heard the song from a new perspective and realized that for months Sarah had been singing about this new ECK Master and telling me his inner name.

Now as she sang, I could hear it clearly: "He is the Master. He's Wah Z." That is what she was singing—not "He was he."

For me, the layers of guidance, direction, instruction, and training we are given spiritually is one of the most fascinating and rewarding aspects of the path of Eckankar. I gained a growing understanding of the reality of the ECK Masters and came to feel a deep sense of spiritual liberation. We ask for inner guidance, direction, and instruction, and the ECK Masters help us in various and unique ways. As we open our hearts to the guidance and love of the Mahanta, this great inner guide, we can receive endless blessings.

I had also learned how important it is that we *ask* for this assistance. If we ask to understand the truth, the answers and experiences will come pouring in to truly grace our lives.

20

A Near-Death Experience:
Inner Guidance Saved My Life

Freud felt that dreams are usually highly distorted because they're protecting the dreamer from unpleasant things. But in ECK* we know that if you open yourself to the Holy Spirit you're going to very often get clear inner experiences. They will tell you in no uncertain terms what to do with your outer life.

—Harold Klemp
How the Inner Master Works[28]

---

*O*ut of the darkness, I saw a red truck barreling down the highway, swerving erratically from side to side. The driver appeared to have lost control completely. The truck careened off the far side of the highway and disappeared over a mound on the other side.

Certain the truck must have crashed, I pulled over. It was night. I didn't want to step out onto the pitch-black highway. I left my engine running and turned on the emergency flashers. I sat in my car for a moment

---

* ECK is the Holy Spirit. Here it is used as a short form of *Eckankar*.

or two, filled with misgivings, and hoped someone would come along quickly and recognize my flashing lights as a signal for help.

Then I saw the red truck again. Apparently, it had run into the embankment but kept going. Now it had swung back onto the highway. Yet, instead of braking to slow down or stop, the driver seemed to be speeding up.

Zigzagging wildly, the truck suddenly turned and headed right in the direction of my car.

A collision was unavoidable. I had already pulled off the road as much as possible, so I could only hope my sleeping daughter would be spared the greatest impact. On the narrow Indiana highway there was nothing else I could do; the truck was coming too quickly. This would be a head-on crash.

I braced myself and desperately called to God for help.

The trip was in the middle of spring break. I had enjoyed several days of rest and rejuvenation away from the high school where I taught while my three-year-old daughter, Sarah, spent a little time with her dad, Jon, in the next state. We were now divorced but remained good friends.

That day, I went to Jon's house to collect Sarah so we could enjoy the rest of the week's vacation together. I had a spring in my step and was prepared for a great day.

I stayed for a while to visit with Jon. Then it was time for us to say our good-byes and set out for home. It was growing dark as I gathered Sarah's belongings and loaded the car.

Sarah was buckled in snugly on the seat next to me.

Almost immediately, she fell fast asleep, tired out from a full day. Her head gently fell forward, pillowed against the heavy canvas duffel bag in which her father had packed her clothes. Exhausted and sleeping soundly, my little one rested on her large, heavy pillow.

*T*he back roads of Indiana were narrow and winding, but they provided the shortest way home. Orange cones marking road construction appeared more and more frequently as twilight came. Soon this route would be a wide, open highway, but for now it was like driving through an obstacle course. I navigated carefully past fluorescent-orange barriers, their warning flashers indicating the more precarious areas of roadwork. With caution, I made my way through the enveloping night.

Nothing, though, prepared me for the red truck. In the final seconds, as it inevitably bore down on us, the last thing I thought I saw was an unconscious driver slumped over the steering wheel.

Then it hit—the large, speeding truck against my small, parked car. The impact was ferocious.

*T*he car was thrown down the highway like a toy from the hands of an angry child. My seat broke in half; the back of it flattened and was violently thrust into the rear of the vehicle. The engine and front half of the car trapped my body. Metal and glass hit everywhere at once like shrapnel. My eyes and mouth filled with shattered glass, and blood streamed down my face into my mouth and ears.

I desperately needed to escape the pain of my injured body, but I fought to remain conscious—a mother's instinct is strong; I wanted to hear Sarah's voice. I needed to know she was alive. When I finally heard her calling me, my ears were so damaged that I had to struggle to hear her little, muffled voice. She was not screaming or even crying.

Yet I could not open my mouth to answer.

Unexpectedly, another woman's voice answered Sarah's call. I could barely hear her comforting my daughter. Sweetly, she spoke to Sarah, saying, "Your mommy's hurt, but she'll be OK. You look just fine. Do you want to come with me, and we'll get some help?"

Could Sarah have been spared and not badly injured? I was reassured as the woman continued to soothe Sarah while lifting her out of the wreck: "Come on, Honey, and we'll get you out of here. We will get help for your mommy. Now, what's your name, Sweetie?"

My heart filled with gratitude because she knew exactly what to do and say. She was a kindergarten teacher, I would later learn—the perfect person to rescue my child.

Sarah told the woman her name, and they left together without speaking to me. Yet I heard Sarah tell her rescuer in a loud, pouting voice, "My mommy bleed!" The woman's constant stream of assurances calmed Sarah as they walked away.

As I waited a painful eternity for my own rescue, I suddenly realized I was floating out of my body. What heaven, what peace! Outside my body, the pain disappeared. I floated in joy and love as I rose up, up, and away.

$\mathcal{L}$ess than twenty-four hours earlier, I had an incredible dream that I recorded in my journal. For several years now, I had been studying the spiritual teachings of Eckankar. I had learned that inner guidance received through dreams can lead us beyond difficulties, provide direction and even prophecy, and open the door to greater truth and happiness.

I was learning to practice certain spiritual techniques of Eckankar, and my dreams were beginning to
provide that most important element in life, the thing
most people long for and pray for—inner guidance. I was
elated because this enabled me to learn the best course
in every moment, to know that I was watched over and
protected. This is the grace of God's presence in our lives.

Dreams are only one facet of the teachings of
Eckankar. My dreams often gave me much-needed awareness, coupled with wisdom about how to live my life and
how to prepare for the challenges of each new day. But
I was also receiving inner guidance in my waking life.

Last night's dream had revealed clearly that great
blessings were pouring into my outer life. It was remarkable. I woke up with my heart racing; I was sure something exhilarating had just taken place or was about to
happen. There was no doubt about it. My outer life was
about to change, and the result was going to be a great
blessing.

This is what I'd written in my journal:

I am standing in the gentle waves of a sparkling, aquamarine ocean. The sun is brilliant overhead, but a soft breeze cools the air and sways the
palms. I walk toward the sandy beach where my
spiritual guide is standing. His smile starts in his
eyes and envelopes his whole face. His arms are
stretched out to me, palms up.

"You've won!" he says happily, and I feel the rush
of an ecstatic joy and sense the pure, divine love he
has for me. I am wide-eyed; my hands fly to my face
like a child with a much-wanted birthday gift.

"Thank you, thank you, thank you!" I exclaim.
Then I ask him, "What have I won?"

"You've won the lottery of life!" he replies.

Tears of delight flood my face as I take his hands and express my deepest gratitude. I do not know what the lottery of life is, but I know I want it.

"Yes! Yes! Thank you, I want it. I want the lottery of life!" I reply.

Key to the teachings of Eckankar is an understanding of the Inner Master as one who provides guidance, direction, and protection to all who seek it. This Inner Master is a spiritual teacher who serves both inwardly and outwardly as the leader of Eckankar.

During our dreams, with the help of the Inner Master, we may actually experience the elimination of long-standing karma. This is greatly to our advantage, and learning to work with this benevolent guide is an important step in learning to follow inner guidance. This Inner Master, sometimes called the Dream Master, is the Mahanta. He is an inner guide, the Wayshower available to everyone at all times.

My life was going to change in a miraculous way. And I thought I understood, at least in part, what was happening. Eckankar teaches about the universal spiritual laws, including the Law of Cause and Effect. Each of us, as Soul, has gathered karmic debts that must be resolved as part of our spiritual progress. Somehow, last night, I had taken a big step.

I was liberated. I felt I had paid off a large debt and a new world of wonder awaited me.

The morning after the dream, I had a jubilant feeling of liberation that I could only assume accompanies release of a karmic burden. Also, there was no doubt something important was about to happen. I had learned in Eckankar to connect with and deeply trust the Voice of God that brought me inner guidance. In my dream,

I knew I had connected with the Voice of God.

In a most powerful way, I felt unshackled from something huge, something that perhaps had been impeding my spiritual progress. Could it be true? Had the Mahanta helped release me from an unknown debt? Whatever it was, I knew this represented a major turning point in my life. At the time, I felt I didn't need to know the details; I was simply grateful and deeply relieved.

Before I left home for my trip, I wrote a letter of thanks to Harold Klemp, the spiritual leader of Eckankar. I knew him both as the outer teacher and the Inner Master, and I usually called him Sri Harold. The Living ECK Master is respected but not worshipped. *Sri* is often added to his name as a title of spiritual respect. Sri Harold receives letters from people the world over, and this morning I wanted to write him too. I wanted to be sure to tell him about the brilliant inner experience I had in the dream the night before.

The house was quiet, so it was a perfect time. The night before, I had fallen asleep with a roaring fire and a good book. Now carnelian-colored embers smoldered in the stone fireplace, and a smoky scent filled the room. I relit the fire to counter the morning chill and sat down at my desk.

For several minutes, I sang HU, a love song to God. It is taught as a spiritual exercise in Eckankar. HU is a simple, spiritual song that opens the heart to God's love.

In the letter I wrote that morning, I expressed gratitude for the unseen blessings I could feel winging their way to me. I shared all the details of the dream and confided my new belief that I had won the lottery of life!

What exactly that might mean, I was not sure, but I was certain it was wonderful.

I finished the letter and left it on the dresser in my bedroom, ready to be mailed.

*P*ain pulled at me, and with a horrible thud, I snapped back into my broken body. I was lying in a heap of metal, covered in glass and blood. I realized I could easily pull myself away from this anguish by leaving my body, and I did. Looking down on the scene with inner vision, I saw everything clearly, even though my body was shrouded in rubble and my physical eyes were tightly closed.

From above, I realized that the entire top of the car had been torn off by the powerful impact. The person in the car did resemble me, but it did not feel like me at all. My perspective was completely changed. It was difficult to relate to that injured body, and I realized it was most certainly *not* me, for the real me was floating peacefully above the entire scene.

As I drifted above the wreckage, I felt a question arise from within: Would it be possible to stay alive—live life on earth with my beautiful daughter—and still know this freedom and amazing sense of exhilaration and joy?

Interesting question, I thought, not wanting to put any attention on it. I didn't really know or care. I knew that nothing could compare with what I was feeling now: total contentment. Simply, I longed to stay in this sweet, floating freedom.

Yet my attention was being directed toward the spectacle below, and a second impression came to me: "Look at the scene of the car wreck. Look carefully at what's going on down there."

With a gentleness which I've come to recognize as the presence of the Mahanta giving me inner guidance, my attention was being redirected. I followed the guidance given and turned to examine the scene below. Watching from my perspective as Soul, which at the moment was hovering around the tops of the trees lining the highway, I studied the car wreck. I could see everything in great detail, and I gazed with detachment at the entire drama, looking at it like one would watch a play.

Vehicles were arriving with lights flashing and sirens screaming—fire trucks, police cars, and an ambulance. I could hear many people talking. The injured driver of the truck that hit my car was being rescued. He was unconscious. From my treetop vantage point, with greatly heightened senses, I could smell alcohol all over him.

It made sense now. I suddenly understood what had happened: a drunk driver had passed out at the wheel of his truck with his foot on the accelerator. No wonder the truck, alone on the highway, had been so totally out of control.

How it had careened until it had perfectly aligned itself with my car, I could not imagine. Still, I felt no sense of judgment as I watched, but just a serene awareness as the paramedics and firemen carefully carried the wounded man to the ambulance. I watched the vehicle transport him from the scene of the wreck.

Then my awareness shifted. My daughter! Where was she? Ah, yes, rescued by the kind woman.

And what about me? There was only one ambulance.

Wait! Why had they left without me? Sarah was surely being cared for, and the drunk driver was already on his way in the ambulance, yet there my body lay in the smashed car, still bleeding and motionless. At the same time, I saw a strange sedan arrive on the scene. The vehicle was long and dark with a rounded top. Was it a hearse?

Aghast, I realized the rescue team believed I was dead. I was shocked back into full awareness of my physical body.

"I'm not dead," I cried out inwardly. "I want an ambulance! I want to be rescued!"

*S*everal men approached my wrecked car. One ignited a blowtorch, and I could see that he was going to use it to cut the metal away from my body. The hissing sound filled the night air.

"Careful!" I wanted to shout, "Don't burn my body!"

I suddenly felt defensive and very distressed. I wanted to be with my daughter! I wanted to be with her—and *not* dead.

My thoughts spoke to no one in particular. *They shouldn't assume I'm dead just because I'm not in that injured body. Unless, of course*, I considered, *I* am *dead!* A clear realization pressed itself into my consciousness, showing me exactly what I needed to do. Inner guidance, coming loud and clear now, forced me into urgent and immediate action.

There was no time to lose; Sarah needed me.

I made my intent clear, to the universe and to myself. "I'm getting back into that body right now!" I shouted inwardly. I had a child, and I would not leave her. "I cannot be dead! I *will not* be dead! I am going back, now! I want to live!" I declared.

*F*or the second time in one night, I was flying straight into a torture chamber, and there was no stopping it. The pain was excruciating, and I truly did not know how long I could endure it.

Through the gurgling of blood in my ears, I could

hear two men's muffled talking and the hissing sound of the blowtorch. I grew violently ill and knew I must hold on tightly to stay in this body.

Suddenly I heard a man speaking directly to me, very slowly, loudly, and deliberately: "Can you hear me? Can you speak to me? Come on, Dear. Can you move?" Desperately he added, "Are you *alive*?"

The shattered windshield pressed into my face, and glass splinters were piercing my mouth and tongue. I could not answer his questions. I did not dare to move any part of my face. It felt as if my eyes were also full of glass, and I would not even try to open them. Yet it was critical that I somehow find a way to respond.

"Honey, if you can hear me," he pleaded, "just give me a sign that you're alive; just a sign!"

A sign! How could I signal him? I wondered what part of my body I could move safely. I tried to put my attention on my left hand. I commanded myself to act: "Control your hand!" The little finger of my left hand was sticking up above the rubble. I managed to wiggle the finger slowly, very slowly. In case he could see me, I tried to smile with my mouth closed, forming a weak, desperate grimace. I continued to gently wiggle the pinky finger of my left hand.

He saw the movement. "Dear God, she's alive! She's alive!" he shouted out to the others. Choked up and in tears, he hoarsely whispered, "You just hold on. Sorry we didn't get you out of here sooner. We thought we'd lost you! We're here now. It's OK. Just hold on!"

21

In the Heart of God:
Inner Guidance to Sing HU

The quickest way to put your state of con-
sciousness in the heart of God is to sing HU.

—Harold Klemp
How the Inner Master Works[29]

---

*T*hey began work immediately with the Jaws of
Life, a contraption designed to pry wreckage
apart and provide access to anyone trapped
inside.

"She's still alive! Let's get her out of here—fast!"
Those were the last words I heard as I descended into
the dark peace of unconsciousness.

When I arrived in the operating room, I was shocked
back into full awareness, and I was sick with pain. My
eyelids were stretched open, and my eyeballs were being
flushed with sharp streams of water. At the same time,
they were pulling stitches into the cut on my head.
Simultaneously, while my tongue was held out from my
mouth by some kind of device, another doctor was re-
moving glass, piece by piece, from the soft, bleeding
tissue. As blood dripped down my throat, I gagged and
tried to turn my head. It was unbearable.

A doctor spoke to me sternly. He explained that due to the concussion, they were unable to give me anything for the pain. He warned me not to allow myself to vomit. After shifting from free-floating bliss to unspeakable agony, I could not control the violent response of my body. I gagged again as I struggled to free my head.

"Stop!" he urgently warned me again. "Just hold on; you've got to! Be still and hold on."

But my body had sustained massive injuries. I was bleeding internally and had cracked bones and too many cuts and wounds to count. My head felt like it might explode, and each throb of blood through my swollen temples brought a new wave of severe nausea. It almost made me faint, but they kept bringing me back. Suddenly, I was struggling even to breathe.

"We're losing her!" a nurse called out.

Through all the pain, I still knew that the responsibility was mine. I knew what to do, and I had to do it. I had to switch my attention to the Mahanta and my inner guidance. I cried silently, sending an urgent distress call to the Inner Master: "I need you now more than ever! Help me. Now, now, please, now! Tell me what to do."

"Sing HU." It came as a distinct impression, a powerful inner communication—inner guidance so strong it was as if I was a receiving tower picking up a direct message from the universe itself. I heard it loudly, clearly penetrating my pain and misery. I was being directed by my inner guide, the Mahanta, to sing HU, a prayer of the highest sort, which I often sang as part of my Eckankar spiritual exercises. Of course! I knew and understood this. I could help uplift the entire scene by simply singing HU.

But I could not sing. My tongue was still held tightly in the surgical vice.

*S*ince I could not sing aloud, I *thought* the word HU silently in my head. Then, when the last piece of glass was removed from my tongue and it was suddenly freed, I weakly whispered, "HU." Tears poured down my face as I sang HU as loudly as I could and the hoarse sound filled the room.

"HU-U-U-U."

The doctor who had admonished me to be still and hang on was continuing to remove glass from my face, but he had finished working on my eyes. I could now see him, despite the tears. I began to let go of the tension and pain as I sang HU, and I looked into his face, imploring him inwardly to join me. Suddenly, I heard him encouraging me.

"HU, HU," the doctor called out. "You just keep singing that word. I don't know what you're doing, but just keep it up! That's it, Sweetheart," he urged. "It's helping. That's better." I was much more relaxed; I was breathing more easily now and felt some relief. He picked up the chant, "HU-U-U-U." As he sang along with me, he encouraged the others to do the same.

"Sing," he urged the other doctor standing by my head. And to the nurses in the room he said, "Sing!"

A nurse yelled, "She's stabilizing." She called out my vital signs, and a little cheer went up. "Keep it up! You're doing a lot better," the nurse encouraged me. Then she joined in the song of HU.

Everyone was singing it. The room filled with the sound of HU.

I sing HU every day. I know its many benefits. Like an Olympian's training serves him in times of competition, in this crisis, my daily spiritual practice was serving me well.

This sacred name of God, HU, reverberated through my very being. Resting quietly on the table now, I no longer felt the pain. I sighed with relief. I felt happy and relaxed although I was fully aware of all the desperate activity going on around me. I smiled and gently whispered HU, and then left the chanting to the rest of them.

"Smiling! Can you believe that?" exclaimed the doctor who was standing just above my head. He continued to sing HU while he proceeded with painstaking care. I relaxed and let them do their work while the entire room filled with this holy sound.

$\mathcal{O}$ver the gentle chanting of HU, I could hear my daughter's voice in the hallway, just outside the operating room of this little country hospital.

I heard her demanding to see her mommy. Sarah sounded fine. I smiled at her brashness. I had not seen her since the wreck, and she had not seen me. I asked if Sarah could be brought to me. I wanted to see her and reassure her. I knew she wouldn't be disruptive, and the doctor agreed it was a good idea. Shortly, they brought her right into the operating room, "flying" her small body over my chest. It took four people, each one holding a little arm or leg. They all were laughing, including Sarah, as she "flew" into the room.

Looking down on me from above with a frown, she asked, "Are you OK, Mommy?"

I assured her that I would be fine soon. I could hardly believe my eyes. She appeared totally unharmed but was dismayed, even indignant, to see the shape I was in.

"Mommy, you bleed, and you're dirty," Sarah admonished.

"I know, Honey, but they'll clean me up. I just got hurt a little," I whispered. "You're not hurt at all. How did you end up looking so good?"

"My bag of clothes went over me, Mommy."

The oversized duffel bag of clothes had been stuffed between the dashboard and the seat, directly in front of Sarah. On impact, the open bag had been forced over her like a protective cocoon. She had sustained only one small cut on her back, which had been treated readily— a quick suture or two, and she was fine.

The nurses told me that Sarah's dad was on his way to collect her, and he would take her with him. I would remain in the hospital. I hated having Sarah taken from me, but I was in no condition to object or to take care of her.

Once Sarah left the room, it was time to resume treating my injuries. My ear was cut deeply from behind, and my head still needed more stitches. As they began, the doctors told me I would have to remain completely still. It took no great effort at this point, because I felt calm and relaxed.

The doctors knew just what to do. They sang HU to me as the cleanup continued. Even I was surprised that I felt no pain. I could sense their hands and equipment touching me, and I could feel pressure, but it did not hurt at all. Throughout the process, from this point on, I was relieved from the excruciating pain and was able to respond easily to the doctors and nurses who attended me.

I awoke in a private room in the hospital, with a dull throbbing in my head and every part of my body. I slowly opened my eyes. Standing in front of me were two doctors and two nurses from the operating room.

Once we had exchanged brief greetings and pleasantries, they said they had some questions for me. Of course, I thought they intended to ask something about the wreck or how I was feeling after last night's ordeal. I was mistaken.

After a very brief exchange about my health, they plunged into their questions. They wanted to understand what had happened in the operating room the night before—especially about the technique we had used, singing the word *HU*. They checked the pronunciation with me. Yes, they had it correct: It is H-U, a two-letter word, and is pronounced like the word *hue*.

They had a laundry list of things they wanted to understand. What is HU? Where did this word come from? How does it work? Where does it get its power? How does one know when to use it? How had it provided such a calming effect, eliminating pain and helping so effectively in the operating room?

Oh, where to begin? Although I was happy to tell them about the HU, I answered haltingly. "HU is an ancient name of God," I said. "Singing it on a regular basis raises the vibration of the body and enhances the consciousness. It's known throughout the world and is often used in the Spiritual Exercises of Eckankar. I've studied this teaching for several years and learned to sing HU as a daily spiritual exercise."

They pulled up chairs, obviously interested. They'd clearly never seen anything like the effect of singing HU and were intrigued by what had happened in the operating room. As we continued to talk, I admitted I was also impressed.

I shared the Eckankar perspective that life is a school for each individual, where he or she learns to live in creative harmony with all aspects of life. And that sometimes the lessons come in unexpected ways and serve our greatest good, even when it does not appear to be so.

And I also told them that when we sing HU, we trust

that we are aligning ourselves with the will of God—whatever that may be—without trying to control the outcome. Indeed, we find that often the greatest blessings may come through hardships, whether we like it or not.

One of the doctors pressed me with questions that he apparently had thought of during the night: "Can we use this word with other patients, or is it just for you? And how do we use it? And when?"

"The HU is for everyone," I said. Again I explained that as a student of Eckankar, I practiced spiritual exercises in which I sang HU daily—with an open heart. This helped me develop a dependable sense of personal inner guidance—which had obviously supported me through last night's ordeal.

"Anyone can sing HU; it's for everyone," I assured them gently. "Singing HU helps you stay in tune with your higher self and connect with Divine Spirit. You can sing it daily, or whenever you need help or want to connect with inner guidance.

"People of all ages, backgrounds, and religions can work with the HU and enhance their lives and faith.

"That does not mean that life will not have hardships when we sing HU. Life's challenges are necessary to help us grow spiritually."

I felt I should add an important point. I didn't want to dampen their enthusiasm, but singing HU means surrendering to God's will. So I said, "You don't try to direct the HU or its power by saying, 'heal this person' or 'take away the pain,' or anything like that. It uplifts and transforms for the greatest good, but we may not even know what that is."

"The results were outstanding. It was so effective!" declared one of the nurses. "I'm amazed we haven't heard of this before."

"I learned to sing HU though Eckankar, which is an ancient spiritual teaching followed by thousands of people throughout the world," I told my little audience. "It is known as a direct path to God. More and more people are hearing about it all the time."

By now, I was exhausted, and as much as I wanted to continue the conversation, I had to laugh and beg for rest. I asked one of the nurses to pull my rescued handbag from a little closet. In it I had a book, *ECKANKAR— The Key to Secret Worlds*, by the modern-day founder of Eckankar, Paul Twitchell.

Still intrigued by the events of the night before, they were totally fascinated. When I said they could keep the book, they negotiated among themselves to determine who would get to read it first.

Before they left, however, they wanted to know more about inner guidance. I mentioned briefly that despite the fact that I had barely survived a terrible accident, I had been *guided* through the entire experience. I made it through this ordeal by using the resources and awareness available to me. They nodded in agreement. I assured them that singing HU could help them develop a greater connection with God.

Having experienced the compelling effect of the HU and the change in the energy in the operating room, they offered no arguments. They wanted this for themselves and their other patients. I clarified that my inner connection had been strong because I regularly practiced singing HU for about twenty minutes each day—one of the simplest Spiritual Exercises of ECK, in which you learn to listen for the whisperings of Divine Spirit.

I assured them that no matter what religion or faith they may practice, singing HU with love in their hearts would enliven their spiritual life. They all seemed eager to try this too.

22

Winning the Lottery of Life:

Inner Guidance on How We Create Our Lives

A little-known benefit of a true Master is his ability to change fate. He has the spiritual power to alter the line of destiny once an individual reaches a higher state of consciousness. If there is enough unfoldment, a true Master will cancel unnecessary karma.

—Harold Klemp
Past Lives, Dreams, and Soul Travel[30]

I was grateful to return to my own apartment. At first, I slept all day and night, barely waking when those who helped care for me came or went. I was slowly recovering, and trying to absorb all that had happened. I had learned much more about the great benefit of listening to my inner guidance and the power of the HU.

Yet, I was still wondering about this entire experience and what it meant.

Some days later, I found the letter I had written to Sri Harold—still on my dresser where I had left it before the wreck. So much had happened since I awoke on that morning, the day of the wreck, and recorded my wonderful dream! I stared for some time at the envelope, then opened the letter and read it.

I was reminded that in the dream I'd "won the lottery of life" and sensed great fortune being bestowed on me.

"Thank you for the great blessings that are about to enter my life," I had written. I couldn't help but laugh at that. Yet I *had* won a "lottery" of sorts—with a huge prize: Although the car accident was not the kind of gift I'd have hoped for, the outcome was a great blessing when compared with the most likely alternative. I had lived!

I had made the choice to live and been given the inner direction to return to my body—and then to sing HU to help in the operating room.

I had also been given inner guidance in the dream so I would know that this was not an accident, but an important cycle of my life. I sensed that old, limiting karma had ended and a wonderful new chapter of my life was beginning.

Nonetheless, I also recognized I had to look further. I had to look more deeply to see the greater spiritual gifts that were a part of this experience—and to discover where inner guidance would lead me next.

I kept a dream journal by my bed so I could capture my dreams each night before I forgot them. One day, as I was dozing during my recovery, I had a vivid dream with Sri Harold, and I jotted it down in my journal. He was guiding me in the dream.

He explained that we were meeting so he could ask

me some questions. His questions would help me realize the full import of my spiritual experience with the accident.

"How old was your father when he died?" the Mahanta, my inner guide, asked me.

"My father? He was young—just in his thirties."

"And how old are you now? About the same age?"

"Yes," I agreed.

"And how did your father die?"

"In an accident. He died instantly in an accident." I sadly recalled the day my father passed away—the sorrow, the unspeakable pain, and the upheaval in our family. I had been eight years old when he died, and I was inconsolable because we were so close.

"And what just happened to you?" the Mahanta gently asked.

A faint light was beginning to dawn. "I had an accident," I said very slowly.

"And what did you wish when your father died?" he prompted me.

Oh, yes, I remembered that part too. "I wished that I could die just like my daddy did. I wanted to go to be with God in heaven, just like my dad," I admitted.

"And what has happened here?" he asked. Then he nodded in my direction.

His final question went unanswered. The Mahanta had disappeared. I woke up.

And what has happened here? The question repeated itself in my mind. My entire being trembled with the answer. I had received the greatest gift of all. The gift of life!

"I know what the 'lottery of life' is!" I shouted to myself. It is another lifetime within this lifetime. It certainly appeared to be a chance to move beyond old karma. It presented a new chance to live, free from past grief and entanglements.

As Sri Harold writes, "People generally don't realize that without the protection of divine love, even the most idle thought creates a karmic situation that needs to be resolved sometime later."[31]

As a child, I had indeed repeated over and over that I wanted to be with my daddy. In fact, I had believed I wanted to die just like he did. I begged God to somehow let me go and be in the heavenly worlds. It did not seem wrong, for in my great sorrow, I had wanted to go to be with him and God. It was as if my beloved father had taken off on a great adventure and left me at home, and I very much wanted to go with him. Never mind that the journey, the great adventure my father went on, was one that we call death.

Yet, I now realized that my words, thoughts, and deep feelings had helped create a mold for my future, developing a scenario that was perhaps first put into place long before I was born. A sense of sorrow had permeated my life for many years after my father's death.

Had I unknowingly drawn into manifestation an accident just like my father's? Was the night of my accident the time that I was going to leave this world? If so, it was only one of the possible outcomes of this life—and it turned out not to be the path I followed.

Through this expanded inner awareness and the Mahanta's gentle spiritual reminders, I now experienced a deeper understanding of what had really happened. I had trusted my inner guidance, and it had led me away from the almost certain doors of death. Because of the guidance and protection I had received, and what I'd learned through the teachings of Eckankar, I felt I'd been spared from my own creation and given the opportunity to write a new future.

This guidance from Divine Spirit is available to everyone, regardless of the path we follow. Through it, our karmic destiny may be changed.

That is what I understood had happened to me. I experienced Eckankar as an accelerated path of spiritual growth in which we can benefit by learning to carefully follow our inner guidance. As our karma is unwound and limitations released, what was once a negative outcome falls away, and new opportunities for spiritual progress await us.

We all face multiple possibilities for the course of our life at any moment. There are choices at every turn. Anytime we go in a certain direction, one outcome is chosen and others are eliminated or avoided. As Soul, a divine spark of God, we have an opportunity to choose. And if we follow our inner guidance, we can learn to make better and more conscious choices.

Through the teachings of Eckankar, everything changed for me. Things were sped up in a perfect way, to move me along steadily for my greatest good.

Tears came to my eyes. I was alive and would be here to raise my precious daughter.

I chose life and had been given a brand-new canvas. The course I had chosen would not be easy; the challenges of life are where our greatest growth may lie. And yet I was grateful for whatever life would bring!

I continued to recuperate in the weeks that followed, and one day a very special card arrived.

Sri Harold Klemp had received the letter I had finally mailed about my lottery dream, with a note at the bottom about the car wreck. He wrote lovingly and told me how glad he was to hear that I had been open to the love and protection of the Mahanta.

He assured me I would see the blessings unfold in my life in many ways. Indeed they were evidenced in many ways in the weeks and months that followed, and they have been demonstrated many times over in the years since.

To receive the blessings, we listen to the inner guidance we are provided. Receiving the gifts has to do with listening and being willing to follow that wisdom.

A few months after the car wreck, life changed dramatically for me. Eckankar, my spiritual path, had sent out a mailing; the international organization was taking applications for a new editor of publications. I had a strong inner nudge to apply, so I did and was offered the position.

Thus ended my teaching career. Sarah and I moved to California, where I took the position in the Eckankar publications department. The change to a desk job was good; my back was badly injured from the wreck, and I needed time to heal.

It was not easy, though. I was grateful for the new job, but the move and my injuries had brought a message home to me clearly: I was quite alone in the physical world. I had wonderful inner guidance and a rich spiritual life, yet at this point I was divorced, with a small daughter to care for and no one to help me with daily demands. My family lived far away and were busy with their own lives.

Feeling sorry for myself, I knew I needed help. Once again, I turned to the Inner Master. I asked for specific inner guidance—to be shown the way to create a strong family of my own that would stay together and sustain, love, and support each other.

A new perspective is what I needed, and to remain open to the support of the Inner Master. My outer life had changed, but now I needed to make it a happy one.

$\mathcal{W}$eeks later, I had a little conversation one day in my office with the Living ECK Master and spiritual head of Eckankar, Sri Harold Klemp. He made a rare visit to my office to talk about an upcoming issue of a quarterly newsletter for members of Eckankar. When he came in, I briefly showed him the article and page layout in question, and we made a minor decision together. It hardly seemed to have warranted a physical meeting, but I was very grateful for the opportunity to work with Sri Harold.

Just as we finished the business at hand, he looked at me, smiled, and quietly said, "Anne, you have a *wonderful* family."

I simply shook my head no.

He responded quickly, without hesitation, and with even more enthusiasm than the first time: "Anne, you have a *wonderful* family!"

Filled with chagrin, I frowned at him. I had thought Sri Harold knew me, knew who I was. He had met my daughter, and he talked with me in the course of my work. Yet now it seemed that he did not know my personal situation and perhaps did not even remember who I was. *Apparently he doesn't,* I thought. It was a humbling experience, and I felt embarrassed.

He looked at me, smiled, and quietly said a third time, "Anne, you have a *wonderful* family."

Disappointment washed over me in a wave. With an acute sense of shame and sorrow, I contradicted his observation. "Actually," I said, "I *don't* have a wonderful family, Sri Harold."

Before I could offer any words of explanation, he repeated, "Anne, you have a *wonderful* family!" He responded with even more enthusiasm than the first time.

What could I expect? I thought. *He has so many responsibilities—so many students of Eckankar who share information with him. How could I expect him to remember the details of my life? Silly me!*

But it was OK. I would gently explain and let Sri Harold get on with his work.

Sighing, I began, "Sri Harold, I *don't* have a wonderful family. I am a single, self-supporting mother on my own with my daughter, Sarah, and I am doing my best to create a lovely little family, but it is not easy. I'm not even dating anyone special, and all my relatives are way across the country. I never see them that much. I am quite alone with just my daughter to raise on my own."

A sense of loneliness enveloped me as I expressed the facts, and the picture of my sad little situation overwhelmed me. Tears welled up in my eyes, and despite my best efforts, they trickled onto my cheeks.

Sri Harold did not speak for a moment. Then he took a deep breath, smiled, and said, "Anne, you have a *wonderful* family."

Didn't he hear me? Didn't he understand what I was saying? I felt like putting my head on the desk and just weeping. What was I not getting? A communication breakdown for sure. I was not certain how to resolve it.

Wiping away my tears, I calmed myself and gently persisted in trying to remind him of my state of affairs. "Remember me, Sri Harold? Divorced recently, all on my own, self-supporting, no family around, just me and my little daughter. That's my situation, and as much as I would love it *not* to be true, it is. I'm sorry; I don't understand what you are saying, because I simply *don't* have a wonderful family."

Sri Harold almost seemed to giggle. "Anne, you *do* have a wonderful family," was all he said, and he seemed to be trying to suppress a big grin. In the face of all my protests, apparently he was going to hold steadfastly to this one positive line about my wonderful family.

Slowly, it began to dawn on me. I knew this spiritual principle taught in Eckankar: if you can imagine a thing and hold it in your heart, it can become real in your life. The Master was very patiently reminding me of this spiritual truth.

A spark of insight began to seep into my heart. The Mahanta had heard my plea for guidance and insight, and now he was supplying it in the best way possible. I had already received inner guidance through Golden-tongued Wisdom. I had received it through dreams. I'd also found it in the Eckankar writings. Here I was now, in an incredibly wonderful moment, receiving guidance from the Living ECK Master himself. He was speaking wisdom to me and teaching me spiritual law.

Harold Klemp, this respected spiritual teacher, was showing me how to create my *own* world with a beautiful, wonderful family!

Quickly, I returned his smile. "Are we *creating* something here?" I asked.

He smiled at me and nodded, and I asked him, "Are we creating a wonderful family? Are we acknowledging a possibility for a wonderful family that is out there in the ethers somewhere? I am all for that!"

Sri Harold looked well pleased as I continued. "OK," I agreed, "I have a wonderful family!"

I was being shown how to place my attention on what I wanted in life, rather than what I did *not* want, regardless of my current situation. I had seen my desires and goals as a *future* possibility. Yet he saw it as real, right now, in this present time and place, regardless of any contradictory circumstances that I might have been holding on to. He paid no heed to my misunderstanding or need to make it a complicated matter. He went for the truth he was presenting and stuck with it.

"Yes," he replied, "you *do* have a wonderful family, Anne."

"Yes, I do," I agreed, with more enthusiasm than before. With rising confidence I added, "I have a *wonderful* family!"

This time he laughed loudly, and so did I. As he left my office, he added a final confirmation. "Yes, yes," he said and paused. He looked me straight in the eyes as he repeated, "Yes, you do have a *wonderful* family, Anne."

The ECK Masters can guide us inwardly and outwardly, and I was being guided to a new perspective, a new state of awareness. I knew the experience was extraordinary, especially because it was occurring outwardly. It was unusual to be guided outwardly by the Living ECK Master one-on-one, but there was nothing unusual about being guided, for he also speaks to us at seminars and through his writings, inwardly in our dreams, and in our awareness, moment by moment. Many times since, I have been guided by his words, his stories, and his gentle inner nudges.

It was the simplest of conversations, if you could call it a conversation at all. Sri Harold had spoken the same few words over and over again—nothing else really. He was guiding me gently but directly. No explanations, and yet I knew my life was changing. In that short time, he had taught me about an important spiritual law, the Law of Attitudes. And oh, the silly resistance I had put up!

While I had argued for my limitations, Sri Harold had taught me to laugh in the face of apparent circumstance, and to speak only the best. In those few moments together, we lived as if the best possible outcomes were already true, and he kept our focus there. We spoke with gratitude and feeling. It was not complicated or difficult; it was masterful.

"Yes, you do have a *wonderful* family, Anne." That is what he had taught me.

For me, it was about taking responsibility for my own life, to create the greatest good. He did not lecture. He did not even encourage. He went straight to the heart of the matter. He addressed my belief, my attitude. I was previously expecting and experiencing the worst—and he turned that all around.

I persisted in contemplating my joyous situation and my wonderful family. The consequences were astounding. Where I had experienced difficult relationships in the past, now that all fell away.

Without drama, the discord vanished as if it had never existed. From my point of view, that was a miracle.

Following this meeting with Sri Harold, I continued to ask for guidance and direction and received much in the process. In short order, all the strained relationships of my past were healed, through many different circumstances. I never even wondered how it might happen; I just held the belief that it would, with the great certainty Sri Harold taught me. Joy and optimism followed.

It is quite interesting how such a simple step in the direction of a new vision of life can be so powerful. For me, it changed everything.

$\mathcal{I}$t was truly a release of karma that day, for me. I was given direct guidance on how to leave behind the sorrowful ending of my first marriage and career, to heal at a deeper level than I could have imagined.

For each of us, the Mahanta, the Living ECK Master is willing to hold a picture of our greatest and highest potential as Soul. He will help us get beyond the limitations we have accepted for ourselves and remind us of the vast possibilities awaiting us, both spiritually and outwardly in our physical lives. He helps us move beyond previous limitations, love ourselves as Soul, and expand into greater states of consciousness with new and more wonderful experiences.

Sri Harold writes, "The test of any true religion is this: Does it help people into a greater state of consciousness and does it help them find love?"[32] Eckankar works for me because it does exactly that—each and every time.

These days, there is no doubt: just as predicted, I do have a *wonderful* family in every sense. We are many, and all very close. I have been very happily married for over twenty years to my dear husband, Alden, and my life is replete with joy and blessings. Loving family, children, and friends surround us, and life is beautiful. As we walk through our days now, our lives are full and rewarding.

Life is good—and my family is wonderful.

23

Welcoming Healing and Health:

Inner Guidance Provides Protection

Through the Spiritual Exercises of ECK, you can keep aware of the hints and nudges and whisperings of the Holy Spirit as It tries to guide you to the next step to take at any given point. One of the things you learn is that there is always a way. Always.

—Harold Klemp
Cloak of Consciousness[33]

---

lden and I had been happily married for six years. We both recognized the significance of inner guidance and how it came through our dreams.

Alden nudged me gently: "Anne, can you remember any dreams?"

"Yes, I keep having the same dream over and over," I answered from a fog of fever and exhaustion. "It's a village in Africa," I whispered. I closed my eyes, trying to recall the painful dream that had haunted me through this week of illness. "I am stretched out on a low-lying cot in my village. I am dying."

I asked for a drink of water and then continued. "I'm in a small hut, hot and humid, the air acrid, heavy, and filled with the stench of death. I am a native of the area, a small woman with very dark skin. Everyone around me is dead. I may be the only one left in the village."

Alden pressed my hand with urgency and asked, "What else do you remember?"

"It's malaria," I said. "The worst malaria we have ever seen."

Alden and I were both perplexed by the terrible health condition that was plaguing me. Alden had an inner nudge, a form of inner guidance, that my dreams might possibly hold a clue to understanding the life-and-death struggle that was before me.

Slapping my bare arms to ward off the unwanted pests, I moved closer to the blazing campfire. It was a hot night, but everyone at the campout welcomed the fire. It lit the dark night and added gaiety to the gathering of youth and parents. The fire also protected us from the damp night air of summer in Iowa, and perhaps it helped keep away the bugs. The mosquitoes seemed to be everywhere.

That night, we sang and ate dinner by the campfire until I begged to go back to our bunk. I was unusually weary. I told myself I was just drained by fun and sun. I needed a good night's sleep.

But back in the cabin, I knew something was not right. I was shivering in the gentle breeze from the fans, and the air flow bothered my skin. On that hot night, I put on my warmest clothes, curled up under a blanket, and went to sleep.

It was almost daylight when I awoke, drenched in perspiration, my heart beating hard, in pain throughout my body, with shivering chills that caused my teeth to chatter.

"Alden, I think I have the flu," I said. "I feel horrible. I need to go home."

"Maybe some breakfast would help," my husband suggested.

Food was the last thing I wanted. And after feeling my blazing forehead, Alden realized he had better take me home as soon as possible. Our daughter, Sarah, would stay and return later with friends.

Alden packed up everything, and we headed home.

Days passed as I lay in bed with the flu. Healing requires rest and time, and we applied the standard treatments—drinking plenty of liquids and staying in bed. I had also taken natural remedies, sipped chicken soup, and slept a lot. We assumed I would soon recover.

But I didn't. A week passed, and the fever persisted. I grew weaker. Some days I thought I was improving, but soon I stopped eating and could only sip liquids. Sometimes even liquids would make me ill.

My husband was getting very concerned. It was over ninety degrees outside in the middle of a scorching summer, and I was in bed, freezing, with blankets piled up many layers deep.

"This flu has gone on too long," Alden told me quietly. "I need to call the doctor or drive you in to see him."

"Can't go anywhere," I said. "I'm too cold."

He leaned down and held his worried face close to mine. "That's exactly what I mean," he said. "I don't know how to make it easy for you, but I am sure I have to get you out of here, Annie."

I said, "Just call the doctor and ask if there is a flu bug that lasts about a week, accompanied by a fever. Tell him I feel like I was kicked in the back by a horse." I imagined the doctor would say, Yep, that's the "Kicked in the back by a horse" flu, and it will go away tomorrow.

Alden dropped down by my side and asked me a couple of questions—not about my symptoms, which we had discussed all week, but something more unusual. Again he asked, "What about your dreams, Anne?"

"It's just a nightmare," I said. "I'm just dreaming about what's going on here. I am sick and miserable." I related the African village dream scenario again.

Alarmed, he put his hand on my hot forehead. "Malaria? You're dying of malaria?"

"Yes, in the dream I am. Not here. Only in the dream, Alden. Here I have the flu, but in the dream it just feels the same." I tried to reassure him, but my confidence was waning.

Alden shook his head. He placed the call to the doctor.

"We have to go to the clinic right away," he told me. "The doctor said we should have come sooner. There is no flu like you described."

Wearing flannel pajamas, thick socks, and my winter coat, I left for the doctor on this hot summer's day. When I arrived at the clinic, they did tests and asked questions.

"Have you been out of the country?" the doctor demanded.

"No," I shook my head, my teeth chattering. "I haven't been out of the country in years."

"Where have you been?"

I screamed in pain as he touched my aching back.

Alden replied, "We've been to a campout in Iowa with lots of other people who are fine."

"Nowhere else?"

"I think I know why you think I've been out of the country," I said slowly. "You think I have malaria, don't you?"

The doctor looked at me. "Why would you say that?"

"I keep dreaming about having malaria, and now I think that somehow I really do have it."

He nodded. "I think so too. Have you ever had malaria before?"

"No, I never had malaria or anything like this."

Sternly he pronounced, "I just don't know how on earth you could have malaria from going on a camping trip to Iowa. We will have to send you to the hospital for more tests, right now."

$\mathcal{T}$he doctor and two nurses were waiting for us when we arrived at the hospital. This was totally exhausting, and all I wanted was to sleep.

They determined I was severely dehydrated, so they hooked me up to multiple IVs. Then the diagnosis came back: I had indeed contracted malaria. No one seemed to know how. The tests continued.

Could there be more involved than malaria? Blood was drawn, and more blood. Then the doctor came in with a startlingly long needle. We learned that part of the course of investigation into my illness would be a spinal tap. The sight of the needle hinted at how painful this process might be, but the doctor insisted it was necessary to test further. Left undetected and untreated, other diseases I might have were capable of ending my life in the next twenty-four hours.

I felt like I was slipping away, as I had in that dream of Africa. Yet I was not alone, and now I knew I could call upon God and the Inner Master for guidance and protection. I had so much left to do in this lifetime! I was sure of it.

Inwardly, I began to allow the sound of HU to roll through my heart and mind, and the holy Sound sent waves of love through me.

The doctor began to explain the process of the spinal tap. The long needle would be inserted into the spinal canal in the lower back to collect cerebrospinal fluid for laboratory analysis. Though they were sure I had malaria, a parasite infecting my blood, they were also testing for meningitis and encephalitis and other possible infections. The doctor stressed the urgency to proceed, and despite the ominous needle, he did not feel it would be painful.

Fever, fear, and nausea were overwhelming me. I felt I was losing my fragile hold on life. The nurse helped move my body into the correct position for the test: I had to crouch on the table and then curl forward with my knees tucked under me to best expose my spine. My back hurt badly, and it was hard to breathe.

Silently I sang HU and tried to relax. The needle insertion began.

Unbearable burning seared through my back! The pain was excruciating. How could anyone say this was not painful? And, perhaps worse yet, no spinal fluid was forthcoming. None. The doctor reassured us he had successfully done this procedure many times. He would try again.

As the needle entered the area of my spine again, my leg flew out uncontrollably in a violent spasm, and

I shook all over. The pain was unendurable. The doctor had hit a nerve, and I felt it throughout my body. It was the worst pain I had ever experienced in my life.

The doctor tried again. More spasms and pain like a violent electric shock. Still no fluid.

I was certain I could not stand another failed attempt. I turned my head slightly and glanced at the doctor. A trail of perspiration was pouring down his face. He stood there with another long needle and appeared nervous and upset.

I began to faint, flickering on the edge of consciousness. I saw myself like a small burning candle whose flame could easily be extinguished by the most gentle breeze. Alden held my hand and stroked my face, and I felt his love, but I knew I was indeed lingering between two worlds.

Inwardly I felt warned. If I were going to live through this, something would have to change for the better— and quickly.

$\mathcal{I}$ heard the inner voice like a single note of music—clear inner guidance: "Sing HU."

I was being guided to surrender to the loving care of God. Here we were with strangers in a life-and-death struggle, yet it was time to rely upon this primordial sound and its uplifting vibration. It was time to introduce this doctor and his team to the power of the ancient sound of HU.

I whispered weakly, "We have to sing HU, Alden."

Alden nodded.

"We have to stop and sing HU," I repeated. "No more stabbing, please. I won't make it if he continues. We need guidance. We can ask for guidance."

The sense of fear in the room was tangible. Everyone was worried and had been from the moment I arrived.

There was no cheerful repartee or reassuring. And now, with the failed attempts at the spinal tap, it was worse. Alden sweetly kissed my hand. Then he began to explain to the doctor and nurses about the HU, asking them to please be aware and let us know if they gained any guidance in the process. They all nodded.

"HU-U-U-U," Alden sang, slowly and clearly. "HU-U-U-U." I joined in softly for just a moment, and then the doctor and nurses began to sing along.

As the holy sound of HU reverberated off the stark walls and the stainless-steel equipment in the room, I felt a moment of true peace. Suddenly everything seemed sacred. I was reassured as the sound of HU filled this medical emergency room.

Shortly, the HU faded away, and we remained in silence after Alden spoke these words: "May the blessings be."

"You must know your exact intentions," I whispered. It was the inner message I'd just received. Yet it was beyond my comprehension in that moment. I asked, "What's an intention, Alden? I can't even remember."

Alden leaned in closely and said, "Our intentions are whatever we want to have happen. So we have to know our exact intentions—exactly what we want to have happen?"

"Yes, that's what I heard," I said. "But I don't know what our exact intentions are."

Suddenly the doctor interrupted. "I do," he enthusiastically responded. "I know our intentions. I know exactly what we want."

"Please tell us. What do we want?" Alden asked.

The doctor rolled a cart next to Alden, placing it in my field of vision. On the cart were quite a few tall, thin glass tubes, held upright in a wooden frame. "We need these tubes filled with fluid," he told us.

The tubes were so tall, the needle so big. I was so dehydrated, my lips parched and dry.

"You want those vials *filled* with fluid?" Alden inquired.

"What I actually mean is that we need just a little bit of spinal fluid in each tube for the separate tests," the doctor explained.

"What will it look like?" Alden asked.

"Pink?" I offered.

The doctor shook his head. "It has to be clear liquid, or it is not a good test. It is clear spinal fluid we need. Just a little in each tube—and we can get that from one good draw."

"And then what?" Alden asked. "What are our intentions?"

"Here is what we want to have happen," the doctor explained. "We get the fluid in one draw and test it. We have the results quickly. And we don't find any additional infections beyond the malaria. Then we'll give your wife additional fluids and send you both home— and she'll be OK," he smiled. "Those are our intentions."

Now we knew what we wanted. If this were God's will, I would be well again. It would be different from the dream, different from that other lifetime in Africa. There would be a healing.

Suddenly I felt everything was going to be all right. "OK, Alden, I'm ready," I said. "Just one more time."

The doctor picked up the needle again but then hesitated. Doubt entered for a moment. Fear was trying to get back into the room.

"Perhaps I should get another doctor to come in. I could ask my colleague to join us," he suggested.

"No," Alden and I said in unison. Alden continued, "We sang HU together, and we know what we have to do. You'll be guided, and we trust you."

"All right. I'm ready," the doctor said quietly. He prepared to puncture my spine again.

There was total silence in the room. I sang HU inwardly as I knew my husband was also doing. Then I felt the needle enter near the back of my neck, and I heard the doctor shout.

"Oh, my God!" he yelled, and no one else dared speak. "Eureka!"

"He found the fluid," the nurse whispered. "He found it." She was kneeling in front of me, holding me in place, and I could see her face. Tears filled her eyes as she nodded her head in assurance. "It worked; he got what he needed."

The doctor handed off the precious fluid to another nurse, who filled the waiting vials. Then he put his hand on Alden's shoulder reassuringly.

"What happened?" Alden asked. "Why did you yell, 'Oh, my God!' in the middle of the procedure?"

The doctor shook his head, seeking the words. "Just as I lifted the needle to insert it near the base of the spine," he said softly, "it was as if a large hand covered mine. I don't understand how it happened, but that hand just lifted my hand and the needle to the base of Anne's neck. Never would I have put the needle in there, but I did. It never occurred to me that with severe dehydration, the spinal fluid might have primarily collected near her brain. Yet it was there. The fluid retreated to where it was needed most for Anne to stay alive. I think that's why I couldn't get any fluid in my other attempts. And whatever we did here allowed me to be guided."

"Guided," the doctor repeated in wonder. "That's the only thing I can call it."

The doctor smiled at us with absolute joy. He knew the elation, the utter gratitude and outstanding amazement, of being guided by God, of being steered and directed from that higher perspective, that loftier view that sees and knows all things.

It was malaria that I had, a difficult form of the disease. I would live to tell about it and later journey to Africa to finish the karma that began there.

In Autobiography of a Modern Prophet, Harold Klemp writes:

> When a problem arises that outpaces an ECK initiate's ability to handle alone, he is driven to look outside himself for aid. By placing his attention upon the Mahanta, he calls forth the miraculous power of ECK: then all things are possible. And in that moment of awakening, he realizes that the Master has been with him all along. There never was a barrier of separation to keep them apart, except for the blindness of the seeker. The Master reveals his presence by some means, and now the ECK is on the field.

> The initiate, though mindful that he must undergo whatever ordeal he has asked deliverance from, can now play the role of spectator as well as actor. He is an observer in the audience, watching a scene from his life unfold. At the same time, he is the leading character.

> Spiritually he stands at the peak of awareness. In this high state of expectancy, he absorbs the

lessons needed to avoid a replay of this scene ever again. And life goes on.[34]

I had wanted to go to Africa since I was a child. It began when I was just a little girl in South Carolina, standing by the screen door during a rainstorm.

I stood watching it pour, as if that would help it stop. I wanted to be able to go outside and play but had to wait for the rain to go away.

"The little lions," I said. "Look at them climbing the tree!"

"Lions? This is not Africa," my mother laughed. "There are no lions here."

But I saw them, plain as day, frolicking in the tree. Then they disappeared, and I did not see them again. I would dream about lions throughout my life, and lions became an important symbol to me.

As Soul, I experienced being in Africa that day, transported perhaps by my imagination and inner awareness. And I experienced Africa again in the malaria dream.

One day, about six years after the malaria dream, I received a phone call. I was invited to visit West Africa and speak at Eckankar seminars in Nigeria and Ghana. Africa! It was a childhood dream come true.

Unfortunately, I had been sick during those years since the malaria incident. At first, it had not been so bad—just an occasional unexplained illness. Then it escalated and grew more and more frequent. This time no one seemed to know what was wrong. I had not been able to find a cure or even an accurate diagnosis.

I had seen many doctors, but the puzzle remained. If I worked hard or overdid it, even a little bit, my body would shake violently, and I'd have a sudden fever. The episodes could last for hours, and I would be drained and weak afterward.

But I wanted so much to go—to serve at this seminar, and to see this land I'd dreamed about since I was a child.

I put my attention on the Inner Master, the Mahanta, and asked for guidance. I sat down to do a spiritual exercise, to sing HU and just listen. All was quiet. I fell asleep.

Suddenly, a lion appeared in my inner vision.

This was the inner guidance I had asked for. I now knew that I needed to go to Africa. Something would happen there, something that would be valuable and life-changing.

Alden would accompany me—along with two dear friends who agreed to come. Having them on the trip gave me confidence to accept this opportunity with a joyful heart.

Alden and I consulted an experienced international doctor to determine which vaccinations were necessary and to learn what we needed to do to stay healthy in Nigeria and Ghana. When the doctor heard about the symptoms I had been having for years, she asked if I had ever had malaria. I told her about the malaria experience after the campout.

After hearing my story, the doctor told me about a new drug being given to prevent malaria while traveling. It was also used to treat long-standing types of malaria that were very resistant to treatment. "You may have been walking around with malaria these past six years," she said. It could have been what was making me more and more ill.

She prescribed the new drug for me, and we left for Africa.

$\mathcal{T}$he trip to Africa was out of this world. There are not words to do it justice. We experienced inspiration, freedom, excitement, energy, love, and joy. The people in Nigeria were remarkable—beautiful, wise, caring—and they had the most remarkable experiences to share. And in Ghana, everything was pure love. In both countries, we made lifelong friends and had experiences we would always cherish.

When we arrived home, I was well. A miracle had occurred. All of my symptoms were gone, and I no longer had to take delicate care of myself. I was over my former illness completely.

Opportunities to serve with an open heart are like gems strewn along our path—just waiting for us to pick them up. I was guided to this African experience. It was intrinsically linked to my illness six years before, when I had the amazing past-life dream of being the woman dying in the small village. Inner guidance had led me past the obstacles, through the challenges, into the miracles.

By saying yes to Africa, I had been given a gift that I never would have found otherwise. I felt vital now—years younger and stronger than ever.

It was truly a profound healing on all levels.

24

A Gift of Life:

Inner Guidance
and Divine Love

*When one asks in sincerity, What is love? and
opens his heart, the ECK (Holy Spirit) will bring
the gift that is already there and has been there
all along. But the individual must do the spiritual exercises to stay open to the guidance that
is needed every day to preserve and nurture that
love.*

—Harold Klemp
The Golden Heart[35]

---

*L*ove is the great connection we share with
others that allows us to stay tuned in to their
greatest good as well as our own. Love is a
golden thread that unites us all. Sometimes more love
comes unexpectedly, through trauma or a big change
that affects everyone. This happened with my family.

Twenty years after her dramatic escape from death,
my sister, Debbe, was admitted to a hospital in Atlanta.
She needed another operation for an aneurysm.

By now, I had learned much about Eckankar, the
spiritual exercises, and inner guidance. When I spoke

with my sister, I knew this was going to be a crossroads for her, a step in divine love.

I asked gently for inner guidance to better understand the situation, to know what I could do to help.

Sometimes our guidance comes slowly, sometimes in a flash of illumination. "All life will be different now," was the message I instantly received. I felt guided to share this insight with my sister. I wanted to tell her everything would go really well during surgery, but my guidance was clear. "Debbe, all life will be different now," I said, almost in a whisper.

Debbe did not question what I said, nor did she protest. She said, "I know, Annie."

She simply agreed. At some level, we both understood what we were talking about.

From that moment on, my sister and I entered into a rare, almost ethereal level of communication. Few words were necessary. I reassured her from the deepest spiritual perspective I now knew. I said, "You understand that no matter what happens, and no matter which way things go, *you* will be fine. You will do great, and you will be well and perfect and whole. You are Soul, a beautiful, eternal spark of God. You know that, don't you, Deb?"

I was speaking of Debbe as a spiritual being—that which we all are at the deepest core of our being—and she understood.

"Yes," she assured me, "I know that." She said she knew that everything would be OK, no matter what. I felt calm as I made plans to go to Atlanta and be with Debbe.

My inner guidance had let me know that things would be different, not necessarily that she would be healed. And that came true. The operation did not resolve Debbe's physiological malady. In fact, she was in and out of consciousness for three weeks. During this time, the hospital administration graciously allowed me to stay with her. I was able to be there day and night and tend her, even as she slept. Family and friends joined in this vigil.

Debbe recognized everyone and had a chance to be with all of us. In the third week, she even seemed to be on the road to recovery, and therapy began in earnest.

But I wasn't so sure. I sensed something was about to change for my sister. So I remained with her during this period, and my world became the world of intensive care. There was much to be done for Debbe to heal.

$\mathcal{L}$ove was filling all of us who spent time with Debbe, as we stayed close by her side. And love filled the hospital in an unexpected way, bringing healing on many levels.

I was speaking to the neurosurgeon one morning, and he asked me if I knew the details of what had happened to Debbe twenty years earlier, when she had first developed an aneurysm. Of course, I knew the story, because I was there. He persisted, asking if I knew how the doctor had known it was an aneurysm, since Debbe was unconscious when admitted to the hospital. Back then, they did not have the modern, sophisticated equipment for testing that we have today.

I explained that I had worked with the doctor to help Debbe. "I had an inner experience in which I was able to see what was wrong with my sister," I offered. "I was guided to successfully help the doctor identify and locate the aneurysm."

This tired and overworked surgeon then became lighter and brighter. He asked me to tell him the entire story. At the end, he asked, "Why do you suppose the doctor was willing to listen to you?"

Gently, I repeated what the doctor had told me. He knew I was having a spiritual insight, receiving inner guidance. He said that he had seen this sort of thing before and he was aware that, at that moment, perhaps I knew more than anyone about Debbe's condition.

The physician listened intently and then looked at me with teary eyes. He nodded his head in quiet understanding. Then he told me *his* story.

"The name of the doctor who operated on your sister twenty years ago is in her medical file," he said, pointing to the folder on his desk.

"I noticed it right away because that doctor was my roommate in college. We went to medical school together up North and both became surgeons."

What synchronicity! Twenty years apart, in different areas of the country, these former rommates had each operated on my sister. And now, here we stood, recognizing that we were in a remarkable situation. We talked about what had happened to me and how I had been guided to help Debbe and her first surgeon. As I related how the hand of God had worked so profoundly, both this surgeon and I were moved to tears. The story of my sister's previous miraculous recovery touched this doctor's heart.

Yet he gently admitted that he wondered why God had not intervened this time and helped him more with Debbe's operation. It had been grueling and difficult.

My heart felt like it might break right then and there. Though Debbe was improving, I knew she was not out of the woods. In case she did not make it, I wanted the doctor to understand the depth of the spiritual experience surrounding Debbe's first aneurysm. I could feel the love of Divine Spirit surrounding us as I carefully chose my words.

"Things have come full circle," I said, explaining that God's love and guidance are still working, no matter what happens. "And if it is time for Debbe to go, I want to remind you of the second instruction I received as part of the guidance about my sister: 'In truth, there is no death—only the illusion of death.'"

I took comfort in sharing the inspiring story of what had happened so long ago with my sister, as did the surgeon from hearing it. Debbe seemed to be improving steadily. The doctor sent many of the nurses to me, urging them to ask to hear all the details. I was happy to share the story of God's intervention and guidance, as well as my experience in the ocean of God's love and mercy and what I had learned there.

$\mathcal{D}$ay after day, I told the story to all who came to Debbe's room asking to hear it. Many who came by were open to taking another step toward understanding God's mysteries and amazing guidance. They asked how I had continued to stay so open to the Voice of God speaking to me. How was it possible to receive such clear inner guidance?

"I sing HU, an ancient name for God, as a daily spiritual exercise to keep my heart open to divine guidance," I explained. "HU is a love song to God for people of all faiths."

The love in the room remained palpable. Through this monumental change with Debbe, love was reaching out beyond our family into this larger group. I felt called to let everyone know that all the inner guidance anyone needed, for whatever reason, was freely available. I made it clear that by chanting HU, I was better able to hear whatever God was saying, however the guidance was delivered.

As we talked and shared hugs and tears together, love transcended all beliefs. The hospital was abuzz with Debbe's story, and it seemed to be one more perfect piece in the puzzle of life.

The therapists and doctors would visit each day and ask Debbe, "Do you know what day it is? The date? The year?" Debbe knew these things, and it pleased them all greatly. She was alert and aware.

One day, however, when everyone else had left her room, Debbe looked at me and stated matter-of-factly, "Annie, 1998 was a very bad year."

I agreed that the surgery had been difficult, but I reminded her that this was *still* 1998 and that things were going well. She was healing, despite the complications of her condition. Debbe listened to my protests and reassurance and smiled at me with patience and love. Then she seemed to speak to me from some future awareness.

"Annie," she said, "1998 *was* a very bad year. It was the year I died."

As Debbe looked at me with compassion, tears welled up in my eyes. Her demeanor was peaceful. I understood that her use of the word *bad* was not about her. It would be hard on the rest of us if she left—but not on Debbe. As Soul, there is no death. A gentle, inner-world journey home to God, it is a graduation celebration for the one who leaves the physical body behind. Debbie already knew this; I could see it in her eyes.

I found solace in the inner guidance I had received twenty years earlier: "In truth, there is no death—only the illusion of death."

*A*fter three weeks, they finally transferred Debbe out of intensive care. The doctors said she would be fine; we should start making plans to take her home.

That first night she was in the new ward, the doctor told me to enjoy a good night's rest. He sent me back to the house to sleep in a real bed for the first time in weeks. Friends had been sending cards, and I wanted to write notes to tell them the good news: Debbe was out of intensive care!

Yet when I got home, I could not write the notes. I could not write even one. My inner guidance gently stopped me: "Not yet, just wait."

A few hours later, the phone rang.

We were urged to return to the hospital immediately. That night, Debbe would pass quietly into the other worlds. It was time, and she knew it. I knew it. Guided inwardly, we had both known it all along.

When I arrived at the hospital, the doctors were struggling to save her. I rushed to Debbe's side, but she reached out and implored, "Please, no more, Annie. Let me go, please." Her body was failing her, and she was ready.

As Debbe slipped away on her journey home, those of us who knew and loved her tried to comfort each other in our great sense of loss.

My inner guidance showed me clearly that my dear sister had been given a twenty-year reprieve to find a closer relationship with God. In the intervening years between her operations, she had met the love of her life and had given birth to a beautiful son, and her experiences and relationship with them had opened her heart and mind to greater love and compassion.

That last night, before I left her room to go home to rest, Debbe had whispered, "Teach me one of your prayers, Annie."

Debbe already knew about singing HU and had read two Eckankar books, which she loved, but she remained a devout member of her church. Yet I understood that now she was asking something special of me, something very special.

"You want me to teach you one of my prayers, Debbe? An ECK prayer?" I asked her tenderly.

Yes, she nodded, that was what she wanted.

"You can sing HU," I reminded her. "That's a love song to God that anyone of any faith can sing."

"I want another one. Teach me another one—one I will remember," she asked quietly.

HU is very easy to remember, but apparently Debbe wanted something different, just for her. I didn't know exactly what. I felt this was a significant moment, and for a second or two I asked inwardly to understand what it was she needed. Ah, then the gentle awareness came.

As I do my spiritual exercises each day, I often sing HU for a while and then sit quietly and just see what comes through for me. The day before, while I sat in this quiet contemplation, I had been guided toward a new spiritual exercise. It was so straightforward that I nearly overlooked it. I actually wondered why such a simple little exercise came through to me. Now I recognized the profound wisdom of that gift and felt that, in fact, this was the prayer Debbe was seeking.

I felt it was a special token of love, a gift of healing and love from the Mahanta, the Inner Master.

I began to share it with her: "It's really easy. You just stretch out your ten fingers, then fold them down one at a time and say, 'Thank you, God.' That's all it is. Just say, 'Thank you, God,' ten times as you count off with your fingers. Then repeat it if you want. It's a prayer of gratitude."

Debbe smiled broadly in appreciation. As I left the room, she said good-bye, smiled again, and closed her eyes. In the hallway, I turned and took one last look at Deb through the window of her room. I saw her fingers closing, one by one, as her lips moved silently in gratitude.

"Thank you, God." Her lips were forming the words, ever so slowly. "Thank you, God."

This is exactly how I feel today—full of gratitude for the gift of inner guidance that provided such important prescience, wisdom, and instruction at the most profound moments of my life.

$\mathcal{I}$ dreamed about Debbe the other night. She was young and happy and dressed in a pretty white blouse and flowing skirt. She was walking in a beautiful green meadow, and I was riding by in a car with the window down.

I was so excited when I saw her, and I wanted to stop and get out for a visit.

The driver of the vehicle smiled but shook his head and said we could not stop. He slowed down, however, and I waved to Debbe, who was young, strong, and beautiful again, and very real. I blew kisses in her direction. She laughed, sweetly smiled, and threw kisses back to me. Debbie was alive and well.

I awoke the next morning with the sense of her kisses all around me. I felt great love, pure and dear.

25

Thy Will Be Done:
Inner Guidance and Surrender

*We are learning to work with intuition, which
actually is Soul speaking to us and giving us the
gentle guidance to make our life better. Spirit is
always with us, always guiding, always protecting, always attempting to bring joy and make our
life better, but that doesn't mean that we are
always aware and listening.*

—Harold Klemp
How to Find God[36]

---

*I*nner guidance opens the doors to heaven here
and now—as long as our heart remains open to
receive the blessings, ever-increasing awareness, and guidance that are there.

As I learned more about the teachings of Eckankar,
I came to understand a simple, yet profound spiritual
truth: I am a spark of God, Soul, and I exist because of
God's love for me. I am worthy of all the blessings life
has to offer.

We all are.

All lessons begin with love. We are so loved by God
that there is always a spiritual guide—a guardian angel,

if you will—working inwardly with us to assist us and provide guidance and direction. All we have to do is ask, listen, and follow our inner guidance—not blindly, but with faith.

In high school, I was best friends with a girl named Debbie. We lived close by each other and went to the same schools, first in France and then in Germany.

In Europe, we had the most adventurous and unique experiences and shared an amazing history together.

When we graduated, I came back to the States to attend college. Debbie married and had children, and somehow, with the demands of our separate lives, we lost contact with each other.

Even in this age of communication technology, I could not find her. For over a decade, I searched everywhere. I found many other high-school friends, but none of us could find Debbie.

It seemed inconceivable to me that, if we were both on this planet, I would not be able to find her. I searched for her on many popular Internet sites. I made calls; I followed every lead. Many years passed with no success. I could not find my friend.

Finally, I asked for inner guidance. What must I do to find her?

One of the highest forms of prayer and surrender to God is simply to say, "Thy will be done." This act of surrender is to our highest and greatest good. It is a lesson I have been faced with many times in many different situations.

In my search for Debbie, I finally remembered to say, "Thy will be done."

One day, during my spiritual exercise, I saw inwardly that loved ones are never really apart. Whether we are alive in this physical world or not, we are never separated from those we love. The Mahanta showed me how we are together by a bond of love that keeps us linked.

So in my heart, I held my friend Debbie. I decided to focus on that. This comforted me, and I let go of my search.

Time passed. An opportunity developed for me to make a sizeable step up in service to Eckankar: I was asked to present a series of workshops in Colorado. This was exciting and inspiring to me; it was a chance to put into practice much of what I'd learned spiritually over the years as a student of the Eckankar teachings.

This was a volunteer position, and it would keep me very busy for about eighteen months. I wondered how I could put aside my work obligations. Would my husband pick up the slack?

He was in total accord. We decided to commit to this new project.

The venture was everything I thought it would be, and more. It was exciting, beautiful, challenging, and—yes—also exhausting. One time on the way home from Colorado, I found myself crying on the plane. Another workshop had ended, and it had gone well; as ever, I was grateful and honored to be a part of it. But I was also tired from the months of planning and travel.

The flight attendant noticed the tears streaming down my cheeks. "Are you all right?" she gently asked.

I nodded yes. I had an entire row of seats to myself on this flight, so I just leaned against the window and gently sobbed. When the flight attendant kindly asked if she could get me anything, I shook my head and kept on crying.

This was very unusual for me. In my gloom, I wondered if I had perhaps misheard my inner guidance. Had I taken on this project not in true service, but for some mistaken sense of glory? Was I actually doing what I was supposed to be doing—for the greatest good of all?

"Did I do this for the wrong reason?" I asked the Inner Master. "Is this true service, and did I follow my inner guidance accurately, or go off course? Am I even supposed to be doing this?"

Sitting there, thirty thousand feet above the earth, I asked for guidance, direction, and answers. "Whatever the answer may be, Thy will be done," I said.

Eventually, I managed to sleep.

"Wake up. I want to talk to you," the voice said.

It seemed so real, but I was definitely dreaming. Sitting beside me on the plane, so close I could reach out and touch him, was my spiritual guide, Sri Harold Klemp.

"I didn't know you were on this flight," I said. "I have some things I'd like to ask you."

He nodded. "Yes, I want to talk to you too. All you need to do is continue in abiding love and service," he said. "I will take care of the rest."

Not wanting to miss a chance to ask my questions, I barely took in what he said.

"But am I fulfilling my spiritual goals, my life goals, and my purpose?" I asked.

"I know your goals," Sri Harold told me. "I know even the ones you have forgotten."

I was surprised. "What have I forgotten?"

He laughed at that. "Anne, all you need to do is continue in abiding love and service," he repeated. "I will take care of the rest."

With that he was gone. I woke up.

His comment nagged at me: What had I forgotten? Was it one of the details to be handled with this project? I was careful to double-check everything, and I had wonderful assistance, but things could still slip through the cracks.

In a small journal I kept in my purse, I wrote his message: "All you need to do is continue in abiding love and service. I will take care of the rest." From those words, I sensed that the Mahanta was encouraging me about the workshops. The Inner Master had convinced me that my service was coming from a true heart, and I could continue with confidence.

When I arrived at home that evening, I went to check my e-mail. There was a message from a Web site I had used years before in my search for my friend Debbie.

"Someone is looking for you" read the subject line. A phone number was included with the message. I dialed it quickly. Debbie answered!

Her voice took me back through the years in a flood of love. "It's Anne," I managed to say. "I've been looking for you for years and years!"

"Me too," she laughed. "I don't know how we ever lost each other, but let's not do that again."

As I listened to my beloved friend's voice, I heard the words from my dream on the plane: "I know your goals. I know even the ones you have forgotten." Now I was crying tears of joy. Finding Debbie had been a major goal for years; then I found it just too painful to continue. I had put it aside—surrendered this mission to Divine Spirit.

Now, after so many years, after I stopped thinking about it every day, we'd found each other!

At our first meeting, we talked and laughed and caught up. As if we'd just left off yesterday, we picked up on conversations from almost thirty-five years before. Our shared history came together again like a jigsaw puzzle. What I had forgotten, she remembered. All her questions, I could answer. We made plans to meet again as soon as possible.

Since then, Debbie and I have become a part of each other's lives again in every way. We travel together and share adventures again. It is a great blessing for us to have found each other.

Sometimes gifts come not when we want them to come, not when we think they should come, but when we are ready for them. They are sometimes all the sweeter for the wait.

For me, the Spiritual Exercises of Eckankar are the key to an open heart that welcomes these gifts. The spiritual exercises keep my inner awareness observant and responsive. They are an important part of my path on this journey home to God. They help me choose love over power, listen to the inner guidance all around me, and trust where it may lead.

Every time I say, "Thy will be done," and surrender to the greatest good for all, the ECK Masters—real and loving servants of God—help me take the next step home to God.

26

Spiritual Healing of Limited Beliefs:

From Inner Guidance to Outer Abundance

If the dream teachings of ECK achieve anything, may it be to show people how the Holy Spirit teaches through both Its inner and outer guidance. This lifetime is our spiritual laboratory.

—Harold Klemp
The Art of Spiritual Dreaming[37]

---

*I*n the dream, I was walking with the Mahanta, the Living ECK Master, Sri Harold Klemp. Dressed in light-blue clothing, he moved easily across the flower-laden field in which we walked. He seemed to feel very comfortable with the land and apparently enjoyed long hikes in this glorious place. A profound sense of love and freedom emanated from this Master I knew as Wah Z. I felt blessed in his presence as he spoke to me of our true nature as Soul and the most direct way to return home to God.

"Will I be able to remember all this when I wake up?" I asked.

He smiled but made no reply.

I knew this was one of those special dreams of spiritual experience and inner guidance that are clearer than life itself.

Everything around us was vivid. In front of me was a field that was stunningly picturesque—a carpet of grass and flowers, but remarkably different from anything I had ever seen.

Everything sparkled with a brilliance that I could hardly bear. Yet, inexplicably, it filled me with apprehension and anxiety.

We strolled leisurely toward a subtle line in the grass, a fine line of demarcation. I could see it clearly. Beyond this line, each blade of grass glistened even more, as if crowned with an exquisite, tiny emerald. The pistils and stamens within each little flower also gleamed with jeweled radiance—ruby-red or sapphire, topaz or diamond; or simply luminous—pearly and dusted with gold. Here was beauty and opulence beyond description!

Why was I so hesitant as I looked at this magnificent and wonderful sight? My inner guidance was nudging me forward, but I didn't want to go. Some part of me was entirely resistant to the potential experience that lay ahead.

Stopping in my tracks, I looked to the Master and said, "I can go no further."

"Is something wrong?" he inquired.

"I can't go in there." I pointed nervously to the landscape before us.

"Why do you feel that way?"

"If I go there, it will hold me back spiritually. That is the Land of Wealth!" I exclaimed.

"Does that bother you?" he softly asked.

"Of course it does!" I was surprised he didn't seem

to be taking me seriously.

He laughed lightly. "Oh, yes, I remember when you had that idea about other things too."

"What do you mean?"

He reminded me about my youth and beliefs I had held then—fears I had that God would be displeased with almost anything I might do.

"Foolish childhood ideas," I insisted, "are not the same at all. This is serious." It seemed entirely sensible to be concerned about anything that might hold me back spiritually.

Inner guidance told me not to be afraid, to have courage. Yet there was a fine line between courage and folly.

$\mathcal{W}$hile I was busy defending myself, the Inner Master placed his hand on the small of my back and gave me a little push. I stumbled slightly and stepped squarely into the Land of Wealth.

"You pushed me!" I protested.

"I guess I did," he laughed. "You might as well continue with me now. I have some things I want to show you."

Even in this dream, my inner guidance was working to teach me an important lesson. Something vital was about to happen. Though I still felt resistant, I was also curious to see what the Master had to show me.

"OK," I muttered. "I can't go back now anyway."

Then my inner guidance reminded me, "You are walking with the Master! He will protect you from any snares and dangers that you might feel are lurking within this land."

We wandered deeper into the dazzling landscape.

I grew happier and lighter inside. Seeing this, the Master casually asked me, "Now, why were you so afraid that coming here would hold you back spiritually?"

In my mind, wealth and opulence seemed to signify sin and greed. I thought that was universally understood. Isn't that what they said in church? "It is easier for a camel to go through the eye of a needle, than for a rich man to enter into the kingdom of God."

I halfheartedly argued my point, yet I actually longed to let go of this old belief. I had a good life, a good marriage, and wonderful spiritual experiences. But something was still lacking. It was as if limitations, or limiting beliefs I didn't even know about, were running parts of my life.

I'd asked to be rid of these limitations. I wanted to be completely available in service to God. The Inner Master was helping me face this seemingly small but crippling concept. It was important that I become aware of its enormous consequences in my life.

As we passed over a gently sloping rise, I saw people participating in a variety of activities.

A group sat under a lovely weeping willow on a hillside. The tree shimmered as if tiny diamonds covered the length of its long, narrow leaves and the undersides gleamed with a hint of silver. The branches drooped down, almost touching the ground, and rustled in the gentle breeze. The tree stood near a lake with crystal-clear water that glimmered and glistened with flashes of turquoise blue. The scene was breathtaking.

The Mahanta moved me gently in the direction of a small gathering of people studying and discussing material from books. He indicated this little group and told me they were a Satsang, studying sacred teachings.

A second group was painting and drawing land-scapes as we walked near the lake. I marveled at the colors they used, and at their level of artistic mastery. I felt my last bit of resistance slowly melting away, inspired and uplifted by the people and surroundings.

"Let's go talk with some of these people. I want you to meet them," the Master invited.

As we approached the gathering under the magnificent willow, I felt elated. The people welcomed me with great affection, calling me by name before I was even introduced. Several of them stood up and hugged me, expressing delight that I was able to visit them in this place.

When we left the group, I told Wah Z how surprised I was at the welcome I received. They were extraordinarily loving and friendly.

He raised an eyebrow and smiled as he told me, "Perhaps you're judged by the company you keep!" Then he laughed easily. I smiled as I grasped his humor. Yes, it was an endearing thing to say, but it also contained truth. Indeed, I was in good company.

Next, we walked by the brilliant blue lake. Just then, a group of people came ashore from a small boat. They were all dressed in flowing white outfits, and several of them carried picnic baskets.

They left the boat at the shoreline and began to climb the hill, laughing and chatting all the way. As they moved up the slope, I noticed the boat being gently swept back into the lake. I was about to call out to the picnicking group and warn them to rescue their escaping vessel.

But just then, a woman among them noticed the boat floating away into the bobbing waves. As she called out to the others, she pointed at their craft and laughed. They all ran back down the hill and straight into the lake to recover the boat. Waist deep in water when they reached it, they began to frolic and play. Laughing all the while, they dragged the vessel back to the shore. As they emerged from the water with their clothing soaking wet, they remained relaxed, enthusiastic, and joyous.

I would have been upset to have gotten my clothing wet, but this group had turned it into a happy romp in the water! What a difference between my attitude and theirs. I had been anxious about the boat, wanting to shout out in distress, to issue a warning. But they laughed and turned the situation into a delightful interlude.

Clearly, there was something important here to learn.

𝒩ext, my attention was drawn to a herd of horses, galloping along a ridge. They were behind a pristine white picket fence, but the gate was ajar. Again, I was concerned.

"The horses," I called out, "they're escaping!"

The head wrangler heard my cry and acknowledged me with a friendly wave. He tipped his hat in my direction and smiled.

To my astonishment, he opened the gate even wider. When he realized the horses wanted to go for an unfettered run on the other side of the fence, he seemed to approve and accepted it gracefully. Apparently, people in this place were in the habit of regarding each event as genuinely wonderful, even when things happened differently than planned.

We trekked on, and a magnificent temple near the top of the hillside caught my eye. It was an enormous structure, gleaming with translucent gold, so radiant in the sunlight that it was hard to look at it for long. People were streaming in and out of the temple, and I felt a longing to enter it myself.

As we approached this imposing edifice, I looked around. "What is this place, really? Where are we?" I asked.

"This 'Land of Wealth,' as you call it, is your true home."

"This is my *home*?"

The Master only smiled. I was mystified. How could this place be my home? I didn't think like these people. Nor did I yet feel comfortable in this lavish opulence. All of this was beyond my imagination. This land was breathtaking to be sure—but *home*?

"Take a deep breath," said the Inner Master. "Smell the air. Use your senses."

I inhaled deeply, breathing the air, trying to relish and enjoy the feeling as well as the scent. I took several deep breaths and held each of them for a moment.

At first, I searched for a scent I might actually recognize, and although the air had a sweet perfume about it, there was something else that intrigued me. I vaguely recognized something familiar and wanted to figure out how to best describe it. I breathed in again and again, holding each breath to savor it.

The Master asked me what I sensed. Suddenly my own inner knowing provided the answer.

"It is the essence of *calm*. That is the only way I can express it: calm. It is a deep sense of calm and ease!" I exclaimed.

Wah Z nodded and smiled at me, obviously pleased with my response. "Exactly," he agreed. "That is precisely the essence of this place, your true home, and it is just as you have described. Calm and ease are its hallmarks. You can return here anytime. Breathe it in now, so that you will remember what it is like. Recalling this essence will help you come back whenever you want. It will help to lead you home."

We continued to walk together, talking.

Looking at the Master, I smiled, knowing that I had been given a great gift—and invaluable guidance about an important secret of life.

When I awoke in my bed, I was filled with that same feeling of peace and contentment. The Inner Master, using a dream, had taken me beyond my own limitations to a new state of consciousness, into the Land of Wealth! It was just as Harold Klemp writes: "As the Inner Master I come to [people] in the dream state. I talk to them and meet with them. Gradually they become aware of the secret, inner teachings, through the dream state. Then I can begin showing them there's more to life than they could ever have imagined."[38]

Wealth meant so much more to me now; it meant ease, peace, love, and greater harmony. It meant letting go of limitations and accepting beauty and joy, and it meant home—my true spiritual home.

If I could become comfortable with my place in the spectacular and opulent inner worlds of God, I could release the restrictions in my outer life too.

$\mathcal{W}$ith this new awareness, outer circumstances began to reflect the inner wisdom and gifts I had been given. It was important not to fear success. I had been pushed by the Inner Master to a new level of experience and awareness, and I now could open myself to a larger vision and more abundant blessings—with greater trust of the Mahanta.

If we are to fulfill our greatest spiritual and physical potential during this life, these are important lessons we must learn. Now I was approaching life with a much greater sense of adventure. Traveling in the inner worlds of God and receiving guidance and instruction was positively affecting everything I did.

My inner changes brought new levels of richness—spiritual and material. And soon, important changes manifested in my everyday life. An entirely new aspect of my career began to open to me, and I fearlessly moved into the new career directions, taking on big business projects. I opened myself to new opportunities that I previously would never have imagined, and I was delighted by all the positive changes.

Years later, I still contemplate this inner dream experience for the wisdom and guidance it contained. It is interesting how we can use an experience of the past to take us to a new spiritual level, even years later. Such is the wisdom and long arm of the Mahanta.

As Harold Klemp writes, "The dream state is generally a very easy way for the Inner Master to work with Soul because the fears are set aside."[39]

My dream experience in the Land of Wealth was truly a healing from self-limiting beliefs. I was learning to live gladly with abundance on all levels, as a divine gift to Soul.

27

Life or Death in West Africa:

Inner Guidance in Service to All Life

Things happen to us as the ECK guides us to take a step to make something work out right for ourselves. Sometimes It gives warnings. An alarm going off, for instance, might not be for the apparent reason. It could be the ECK signaling us to be alert, be aware, be on the lookout for other things.

—Harold Klemp
Cloak of Consciousness[40]

The hospital conditions were dreadful—hot and humid, with no air conditioning. At this time of night, it was packed with people. The large doors of the facility stood open, and I could see people sitting, standing, or lying around everywhere, suffering from all manner of illness or injury.

My husband had asked me not to go inside this facility, but "Go in and take over" was the clear message I received.

I stepped over a man lying stretched out, half in and half out of the door. The smell was almost overwhelming as I entered the packed waiting room.

"Take over!" Every fiber of my being protested. I definitely had no intention of doing that. Inner alarms were sounding insistent warnings. They were, however, not alarms telling me to stop. They were alarms urging me to hurry along, be alert, and be careful as I entered the hospital—for there was much to be done.

Feeling unable to stop myself, I walked in and asked to hold the dying baby. I knew it was the right thing to do.

It was the last week of our trip to West Africa. Alden and I had arrived in Ghana earlier that night, exhausted from the previous week of traveling and speaking at the Eckankar seminar in Nigeria. We were looking forward to our workshops and talks in Ghana, but this first evening was just for relaxation.

Our hosts welcomed us warmly; then we sat down with the family to sing HU. This ancient name of God is widely known and highly respected in parts of Africa. Any and all significant occasions may signal that it is time to sing HU together.

When the phone rang, it was startling. It seemed far too late for normal calls.

Our host, Irene, left the room to answer it. Immediately, I was nudged into high alert. I was longing for bed, but suddenly I became aware inwardly that we would need to leave the house and rush to someone's aid.

When Irene returned to the room, her husband asked if everything was all right.

"It will be fine," she answered with a creased brow. "I am going to the hospital."

Addressing all of us, she asked, "Do you want to come with me?"

Alden shook his head. There was no way he could go anywhere. But my two friends and I stood up to join Irene. We women would all go to the hospital together.

"You have to be careful," Alden said to me privately. "You can't afford to fall ill. Don't go inside the building, Anne, please. Maybe you can stay outside the hospital and be supportive that way." He gave me a sweet smile of encouragement, but I knew he was serious.

In preparing for this trip to Africa, we had consulted with an international doctor who prescribed malaria prevention and other medications. The doctor gave us a list of things to watch out for: "Don't eat fresh foods. Don't drink the water. Be careful in the shower—keep your mouth closed. Don't walk in forests or jungles. Don't swim in the water." The list went on and on.

Now I had to add this caution from Alden: "Don't go inside the building."

The call was from a grandmother whose grandson was dying. The child's parents were away in London. The woman was a member of Eckankar, and she had telephoned Irene for spiritual support and assistance. It did not look good for the child. She had already taken the baby to one hospital, where she was told they could not help. She was going to the military hospital now, where Irene said she would meet them.

*A*s we approached the hospital, I felt an inner alarm go off—an inner sense that told me to stay on high alert. It was not an alarm about the hospital and any dangers lurking in it. My sense of it was clear: there was work to be done here. I needed to move into high gear, spiritually and physically, and pay close attention inwardly.

My inner hearing needed to be fine-tuned. I stilled myself and sang HU silently within.

Just walking into this place broke every rule of personal protection. It was anyone's guess what kinds of illness we would be exposed to here; there might well be diseases our bodies could not resist. Normally I'd have hesitated, but inwardly I was sure there was no time for vacillation or protest. A baby was dying, and we were here to help.

The inner guidance was clear: I must go in.

We found the grandmother waiting in a line, holding the baby. Her grandson was small, very dark, frail, and dripping with perspiration. He did not appear to be conscious. He lay in his grandmother's arms with his eyes rolled into the back of his head. Only the whites of his eyes were showing—an eerie testimony to his nearly complete absence from this body. His tiny limbs hung loosely. The doctor at the other hospital could not help him. The baby's veins were too tiny, collapsing in attempts to insert an IV. His lips were parched and cracked. It looked as if he might take his last breath at any second.

I asked immediately if I could hold the baby. The grandmother passed him into my arms as she was handed some forms to fill out.

"Go in and take over," I heard inwardly again. What did it mean? What could I actually do? I had the nudge to step forward and ask for assistance.

We moved out of the line together and into the medical area, where I insisted on immediate attention. A nun came to help us. "Only one person can come with the baby," she said, indicating the grandmother. I looked at Irene and the grandmother.

"We're all going in together," I said. I stepped forward with the child, and the nun reluctantly stepped aside.

We walked into the emergency ward of the hospital through a hallway lined with people in terrible condition—bleeding, crying, and seriously ill.

An inner message of caution alerted my consciousness. "White woman," it said, "be very careful here."

While I acknowledged the warning, I intended to see this through. In surrender to the Divine, I said inwardly, "If you want me here, I will need protection, dear God." Then I began to quietly sing HU and declared that I walked in the Mahanta's presence and protection, as a vehicle of divine love in service to all life.

I knew I must stay centered in this love and protection.

The grandmother was told she could go in to see the doctor. The nun reached for the baby, but I shook my head and went into the office with the child. Irene followed. The nun gave us a stern look but did not protest as we entered the doctor's office together.

While the grandmother began to explain the history to the doctor, I studied the baby. Holding him in my arms, my inner sight and awareness were heightened. A form of inner guidance, this ability to see beyond the physical reality indicates the presence of the Inner Master, the Mahanta. Acknowledging the company of this advanced spiritual being allows us to readily experience God's love and blessings in a very direct way.

Inwardly, I suddenly saw that the baby had malaria and was also dehydrated and starving. *Malaria?* I thought. My well-known disease.

I wondered why he was not already being treated for that disease so common in Africa; somehow they had missed it. Certain it was malaria, I knew this child would be dead very soon if he was not treated for this malady right away. And it seemed I would have to be the one to communicate this to a doctor.

The grandmother was beside herself with distress, and now the nun had brought her more papers to sign and forms to fill out. The doctor continued to listen to the grandmother, but he seemed exhausted and overwhelmed and just took a few simple notes.

I decided to speak up. "I think it's malaria," I said to the doctor. He looked up, startled, from his discussion about dry measles. "It's not measles at all. He's probably been misdiagnosed and treated improperly at the other hospital. What do you think? Malaria, wouldn't you say?"

There was suddenly a light in his eyes. He half smiled and nodded.

"Yes, I agree, actually. I think you are right," he said, addressing me and the grandmother. "Yes, we should give him an IV and treat him for malaria."

"His arms have been abused by IV attempts at the other hospital," I warned the doctor. I showed him the child's bruised skin.

He looked. "We will get the preemie needles and another doctor to assist. We won't be able to use his arms at all."

Suddenly, I spoke from a very spiritual place, far different from my normal state of human consciousness. This was Soul's view. I could see myself dropping liquid into the child, and I somehow knew that liquid was called electrolytes. Part of me was thinking, *What are electrolytes?*

Yet I could hear my voice already saying, "I think he needs electrolytes, by mouth, right now. Don't you, Doctor? Can someone bring some to me? I'll see if I can get him to sip them. And I'll need clean bottled water and something to sterilize the lid. That would be helpful, don't you think?"

The work-weary doctor appeared greatly relieved. He readily agreed and nodded to the nun. Off she ran to get what I had requested. I felt rising confidence that the Inner Master was clearly working with me, telling me what to say and do and giving me knowledge of exactly what was needed.

We took the child back out through the overcrowded emergency ward. A small, empty crib awaited him by a window. The crib and window were both very dusty. The window was open, and a breeze was filtering in, but it had also brought a thick layer of dust and dirt. I knew I would have to deal with this too. A nurse arrived with the bottle of electrolytes, bottled water, and everything I needed. We cleaned the lid and added electrolytes to the purified water, and I began to slowly dribble tiny drops of the mixture onto the baby's lips.

At first, the liquid rolled off his lips and down his chin. One drop at a time, I continued, not giving up. I added the precious moisture to his lips and the tip of his parched tongue. Shortly his lips began to move slowly. Then he held a drop in his mouth. Slowly, I added another, and another—slowly, very slowly.

A European doctor arrived by the side of the crib and demanded, "Whose baby is this?"

The grandmother had gone to the administration area, and I had no papers to authorize the treatments, yet I knew we could not waste any time.

"Mine," I asserted. In a sense, I meant it with my whole heart, for in that moment I had accepted full responsibility for the life of this child. "He's mine. Hurry! We need the IV."

This new doctor looked at me oddly, then ordered, "Put him in the crib. The IV will be here in a moment."

But I could not. It needed cleaning first.

Shaking my head, I handed the child to the nun who stood nearby, and I reached into my purse. In view of all the warnings we got before taking this trip, I had prepared for every possibility. I was very grateful that I had listened to the little inner nudge to be prepared, as my handbag was now filled to the brim with individually packaged sanitizing wipes.

I put them to quick use, dozens and dozens of them, and soon we had a clean little plastic crib mattress. And in short order, "my" baby was in the little bed, hooked up to an IV.

I continued using the wipes to clean the rest of the crib. Then I used them to clean the window frame and finally to bathe the baby. As the vital liquids boosted his bloodstream, I lovingly cared for this sweet child. I started with the top of his head and worked my way down his little body, cleaning him with the refreshing cloths.

Before long, his eyes were fluttering open, and it was apparent he could see me. He did not cry out and barely stirred. He simply did not have enough energy yet, but he was coming around.

Slowly and carefully, I continued the little bath. When I gently lifted his arm and wiped underneath, he looked right at me and then, ever so slowly, began to lift his other arm. He liked it and wanted more! I smiled and cleaned under that arm too with the cool cloth.

He gave a weak little smile. In that moment, I knew he would be all right.

The night was slipping by rapidly. Finally all the paperwork was completed, and the baby was officially registered in the hospital. A nurse arrived and put a nameplate on the crib. "Nat Huson," it read.

I knew that name. A young adult by that name, my daughter's friend, had visited our home in the United States. Our family knew Nat Huson well, though I had not seen him in several years. When Irene and the grandmother finally joined me by the crib, I asked about the name.

"Auntie Irene," I lovingly addressed her, "is this baby related to the Nat Huson I know?"

"Yes, of course!" she said. She grinned widely as she shared the whole story. "This is Nat's son. Nat Huson married and has twins. This boy has a twin sister too. And this is the grandmother, who is helping to care for the babies while Nat and his wife are both completing their higher degrees in music in London right now. That's why the grandmother, grandfather, and aunt are taking care of the twins."

Had I helped save the life of a baby whose father, unbeknownst to me, was a man I'd met years before in a place some seven thousand miles from here? It took my breath away. Irene nodded as if she knew what I was thinking.

Baby Nat Huson's young aunt showed up to take over our watch by the bedside. I knew her too. Cynthia and I hugged and greeted each other, and she took over our vigil.

At dawn, Irene and I went home. Weary to the core as we left the hospital, we were also both quite delighted with the way the evening had gone. We were filled with gratitude.

I showered before climbing into bed.

"How'd it go?" Alden yawned.

"Great, just great," I whispered as I cuddled up next to him. "You'll meet the baby tomorrow. We'll visit the hospital."

My husband didn't say anything; he just hugged me tightly.

*I*n the morning light, the hospital didn't look frightening at all. Nat was in the children's ward, in nice, clean clothes and a charming crib, and he looked much better.

He smiled when he saw me, and it touched my heart.

By Sunday, baby Nat was at the ECK Worship Service with his twin sister. He looked at me the whole time with his big, joyful eyes—and I smiled at "my" baby with tears of pure delight.

*I*nner guidance always brings us to the heart of who and what we are as Soul. It may take the form of extraordinary service, as happened to me in that African hospital one dark night. It may be simple and everyday, as when it helps a person find the right job or best relationship. But it's always here, always available to all of us.

This connection with God is our divine birthright. Why? Because God has provided every blessing and gift we could ever need. We just have to raise our awareness enough to be able to recognize the blessings and know we're worthy of them. Why? Because we are Soul, a spark of God.

It's completely up to each of us whether we use this amazing spiritual tool, inner guidance. It takes attention, practice, and above all, trust—knowing that we're worthy of such a beautiful gift.

Harold Klemp, in *The Living Word*, Book 2, says, "Seize the moment, seize the day—and embrace life with joy and wonder."[41] That's what my practice of inner guidance, through the teachings of Eckankar, has brought me: a life of joy and wonder.

May it be so for you too!

Next Steps in Spiritual Exploration

- **Try a spiritual exercise** on a daily basis. Example: With eyes open or closed, take a few deep breaths to relax. Then begin to sing HU (pronounced like the word *hue*) in a long, drawn-out sound, HU-U-U-U. Take another breath, and sing HU again. Continue for up to twenty minutes. Sing HU with a feeling of love, and it will gradually open your heart to God.

- **Browse our Web site: www.Eckankar.org.** Watch videos; get free books, answers to FAQs, and more info.

- **Attend an Eckankar event** in your area. Visit "Eckankar around the World" on our Web site.

- **Read additional books** about the ECK teachings.

- **Explore an advanced spiritual study class** (or study privately) with the Eckankar discourses that come with membership.

Books

If you would like to read additional books by Harold Klemp about the ECK teachings, you may find these of special interest. They are available at bookstores, from online booksellers, or directly from Eckankar.

The Call of Soul

Harold Klemp takes you on an amazing journey into a world you may have only dared to dream of—the infinite world of God's love for you. More, he shows, through spiritual exercises, dream techniques, and Soul Travel explorations, how this love translates into every event, relationship, and moment of your life. Includes a CD with dream and Soul Travel techniques.

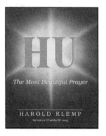

HU, the Most Beautiful Prayer

The simple spiritual exercises in this book will open your heart to see God's loving presence in your life. Includes a CD with the sound of thousands of people singing this powerful, majestic love song to God. Read, listen, or sing along. It lifts you spiritually, no matter your age, background, or religion.

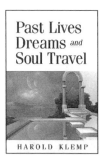

Past Lives, Dreams, and Soul Travel

These stories and exercises help you find your true purpose, discover greater love than you've ever known, and learn that spiritual freedom is within reach.

The Spiritual Exercises of ECK

This book is a staircase with 131 steps leading to the doorway to spiritual freedom, self-mastery, wisdom, and love. A comprehensive volume of spiritual exercises for every need.

How to Survive Spiritually in Our Times, Mahanta Transcripts, Book 16

Discover how to reinvent yourself spiritually—to thrive in a changing world. Stories, tools, techniques, and spiritual insights to apply in your life now.

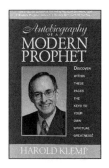

Autobiography of a Modern Prophet

This riveting story of Harold Klemp's climb up the Mountain of God will help you discover the keys to your own spiritual greatness.

Those Wonderful ECK Masters

Would you like to have *personal* experience with spiritual masters that people all over the world—since the beginning of time—have looked to for guidance, protection, and divine love? This book includes real-life stories and spiritual exercises to meet eleven ECK Masters.

The Spiritual Laws of Life

Learn how to keep in tune with your true spiritual nature. Spiritual laws reveal the behind-the-scenes forces at work in your daily life.

Advanced Spiritual Study

Advanced spiritual study is available through yearly membership in Eckankar. This annual cycle of study and practice focuses on the ECK discourses, which may be studied privately or in a class. Each year the spiritual student decides whether to continue with his or her studies in Eckankar.

Discourses

As you study the teachings of ECK, you will find a series of changes in your heart and mind that can make you a better, stronger, and more happy person.

Each month of the year, you'll study a new discourse and practice a new technique to enhance your spiritual journey.

The twelve lessons in *The Easy Way Discourses* by Harold Klemp include these titles and more: "In Soul You Are Free," "Dream On, Sweet Dreamer," "Reincarnation—Why You Came to Earth Again," "The Master Principle," and "The God Worlds—Where No One Has Gone Before?"

How to Get Started

For free books and more information about Eckankar:

• Visit www.Eckankar.org;

• Call 1 (800) LOVE GOD (1-800-568-3463), ext. BK114 (US and Canada only); or

• Write to: ECKANKAR, Dept. BK114,
              PO Box 2000, Chanhassen, MN
              55317-2000 USA.

To order Eckankar books online, visit www.ECKBooks.org.

To become a member of Eckankar and receive your advanced spiritual study discourses, along with other annual membership benefits, go to www.Eckankar.org (click on "Membership" then "Online Membership Application"). You can also call Eckankar at (952) 380-2222 to apply. Or write to the address above, Att: Membership.

Glossary

Words set in SMALL CAPS are defined elsewhere in this glossary.

Blue Light.   How the MAHANTA often appears in the inner worlds to the chela or seeker.

ECK. *EHK*   The Life Force, the Holy Spirit, or Audible Life Current which sustains all life.

Eckankar. *EHK-ahn-kahr*   Religion of the Light and Sound of God. Also known as the Ancient Science of SOUL TRAVEL. A truly spiritual religion for the individual in modern times. The teachings provide a framework for anyone to explore their own spiritual experiences. Established by PAUL TWITCHELL, the modern-day founder, in 1965. The word means Co-worker with God.

ECK Masters.   Spiritual Masters who can assist and protect people in their spiritual studies and travels. The ECK Masters are from a long line of God-Realized SOULS who know the responsibility that goes with spiritual freedom.

God-Realization.   The state of God Consciousness. Complete and conscious awareness of God.

Gopal Das. *GOH-pahl DAHS*   The guardian of the SHARIYAT-KI-SUGMAD at the Temple of Askleposis on the Astral PLANE. He was the MAHANTA, the LIVING ECK MASTER in Egypt, about 3000 BC.

HU. *HYOO*   The most ancient, secret name for God. The singing of the word *HU* is considered a love song to God. It can be sung aloud or silently to oneself.

Karma, Law of.   The Law of Cause and Effect, action and reaction, justice, retribution, and reward, which applies to the lower or psychic worlds: the Physical, Astral, Causal, Mental, and Etheric PLANES.

Klemp, Harold.   The present MAHANTA, the LIVING ECK MASTER. SRI Harold Klemp became the Mahanta, the Living ECK Master in 1981. His spiritual name is WAH Z.

Lai Tsi. *lie TSEE* An ancient Chinese ECK MASTER.

Living ECK Master. The title of the spiritual leader of ECKANKAR. His duty is to lead SOUL back to God. The Living ECK Master can assist spiritual students physically as the Outer Master, in the dream state as the Dream Master, and in the spiritual worlds as the Inner Master. SRI HAROLD KLEMP became the MAHANTA, the Living ECK Master in 1981.

Mahanta. *mah-HAHN-tah* A title to describe the highest state of God Consciousness on earth, often embodied in the LIVING ECK MASTER. He is the Living Word. An expression of the Spirit of God that is always with you. Sometimes seen as a BLUE LIGHT or Blue Star or in the form of the Mahanta, the Living ECK Master.

planes. The levels of existence, such as the Physical, Astral, Causal, Mental, Etheric, and SOUL Planes.

Rebazar Tarzs. *REE-bah-zahr TAHRZ* A Tibetan ECK MASTER known as the Torchbearer of ECKANKAR in the lower worlds.

Satsang. *SAHT-sahng* A class in which students of ECK study a monthly lesson from ECKANKAR.

Self-Realization. SOUL recognition. The entering of Soul into the Soul PLANE and there beholding Itself as pure Spirit. A state of seeing, knowing, and being.

Shariyat-Ki-Sugmad. *SHAH-ree-aht-kee-SOOG-mahd* The sacred scriptures of ECKANKAR. The scriptures are comprised of about twelve volumes in the spiritual worlds. The first two were transcribed from the inner PLANES by PAUL TWITCHELL, modern-day founder of Eckankar.

Soul. The True Self. The inner, most sacred part of each person. Soul exists before birth and lives on after the death of the physical body. As a spark of God, Soul can see, know, and perceive all things. It is the creative center of Its own world.

Soul Travel. The expansion of consciousness. The ability of SOUL to transcend the physical body and travel into the spiritual worlds of God. Soul Travel is taught only by the LIVING ECK MASTER. It helps people unfold spiritually and can provide proof of the existence of God and life after death.

Sound and Light of ECK. The Holy Spirit. The two aspects through which God appears in the lower worlds. People can experience them by looking and listening within themselves and through SOUL TRAVEL.

Spiritual Exercises of ECK. The daily practice of certain techniques to get us in touch with the Light and Sound of God.

Sri. *SREE* A title of spiritual respect, similar to reverend or pastor, used for those who have attained the Kingdom of God. In ECKANKAR, it is reserved for the MAHANTA, the LIVING ECK MASTER.

Sugmad. *SOOG-mahd* A sacred name for God. Sugmad is neither masculine nor feminine; It is the source of all life.

Temples of Golden Wisdom. These Golden Wisdom Temples are spiritual temples which exist on the various PLANES—from the Physical to the Anami Lok; CHELAS of ECKANKAR are taken to the temples in the SOUL body to be educated in the divine knowledge; the different sections of the SHARIYAT-KI-SUGMAD, the sacred teachings of ECK, are kept at these temples.

Twitchell, Paul. An American ECK MASTER who brought the modern teachings of ECKANKAR to the world through his writings and lectures. His spiritual name is Peddar Zaskq.

vairag. *vie-RAHG* Detachment.

Wah Z. *WAH zee* The spiritual name of SRI HAROLD KLEMP. It means the secret doctrine. It is his name in the spiritual worlds.

Yaubl Sacabi. *YEEOW-buhl sah-KAH-bee* Guardian of the SHARIYAT-KI-SUGMAD in the spiritual city of Agam Des. He was the MAHANTA, the LIVING ECK MASTER in ancient Greece.

For more explanations of ECKANKAR terms, see *A Cosmic Sea of Words: The ECKANKAR Lexicon* by Harold Klemp.

Notes

1. Harold Klemp, *How to Survive Spiritually in Our Times*, Mahanta Transcripts, Book 16 (Minneapolis: ECKANKAR, 2001), 11.
2. Harold Klemp, *How the Inner Master Works*, Mahanta Transcripts, Book 12 (Minneapolis: ECKANKAR, 1995), 193.
3. Harold Klemp, *The Secret Teachings*, Mahanta Transcripts, Book 3 (Minneapolis: ECKANKAR, 1989), 103.
4. Harold Klemp, *The Eternal Dreamer*, Mahanta Transcripts, Book 7 (Minneapolis: ECKANKAR, 1992), 7.
5. Klemp, *How to Survive Spiritually*, 79.
6. Harold Klemp, *Cloak of Consciousness*, Mahanta Transcripts, Book 5 (Minneapolis: ECKANKAR, 1991), 65.
7. Harold Klemp, *The Spiritual Laws of Life* (Minneapolis: ECKANKAR, 2002, 2010), 82.
8. Klemp, *How to Survive Spiritually*, 124.
9. Harold Klemp, *Past Lives, Dreams, and Soul Travel* (Minneapolis: ECKANKAR, 2003), 164.
10. Harold Klemp, *The Living Word*, Book 2 (Minneapolis: ECKANKAR, 1996), 17.
11. Harold Klemp, *The Golden Heart*, Mahanta Transcripts, Book 4 (Minneapolis: ECKANKAR, 1990, 2011), 202.
12. Ibid., 31.
13. Klemp, *The Living Word*, Book 2, 204.
14. Harold Klemp, *The Book of ECK Parables*, Volume 1 (Minneapolis: ECKANKAR, 1986), 179.
15. Klemp, *How to Survive Spiritually*, 78–79.
16. Paul Twitchell, *The Flute of God* (Minneapolis: ECKANKAR, 1969), 20.
17. Klemp, *How to Survive Spiritually*, 226.
18. Harold Klemp, *Unlocking the Puzzle Box*, Mahanta Transcripts, Book 6 (Minneapolis: ECKANKAR, 1992), 47.
19. Harold Klemp, *The Art of Spiritual Dreaming* (Minneapolis: ECKANKAR, 1999), 27.
20. Klemp, *The Golden Heart*, 128.

21. Harold Klemp, *How to Find God*, Mahanta Transcripts, Book 2 (Minneapolis: ECKANKAR, 1988), 9.
22. Harold Klemp, *Wisdom of the Heart*, Book 1 (Minneapolis: ECKANKAR, 1992), 49.
23. Klemp, *Inner Master*, 36.
24. Klemp, *The Art of Spiritual Dreaming*, 142.
25. Harold Klemp, *The Slow Burning Love of God*, Mahanta Transcripts, Book 13 (Minneapolis: ECKANKAR, 1996, 1997), 228.
26. Klemp, *How to Find God*, 277–78.
27. Harold Klemp, *Journey of Soul*, Mahanta Transcripts, Book 1 (Minneapolis: ECKANKAR, 1988), 71.
28. Klemp, *Inner Master*, 226.
29. Ibid., 48.
30. Klemp, *Past Lives, Dreams, and Soul Travel*, 115.
31. Klemp, *Inner Master*, 39.
32. Klemp, *How to Survive Spiritually*, 242.
33. Klemp, *Cloak of Consciousness*, 59.
34. Harold Klemp, *Autobiography of a Modern Prophet* (Minneapolis: ECKANKAR, 2000), 237–38.
35. Klemp, *The Golden Heart*, 236.
36. Klemp, *How to Find God*, 277–78.
37. Klemp, *The Art of Spiritual Dreaming*, 283–84.
38. Ibid., 23.
39. Ibid., 141.
40. Klemp, *Cloak of Consciousness*, 125.
41. Klemp, *The Living Word*, Book 2, 204.